CHAMPIONS

CHAMPIONS

The World's Greatest Cricketers Speak

CONVERSATIONS WITH MIKE COWARD

First published in 2013

Allen & Unwin
83 Alexander Street
Crows Nest NSW 2065
Australia
Phone: (61 2) 8425 0100
Email: info@allenandunwin.com
Web: www.allenandunwin.com

Cataloguing-in-Publication details are available
from the National Library of Australia
www.trove.nla.gov.au

ISBN 978 1 74331 561 3

Type design by Darian Causby
Index by Puddingburn
Set in 13/19 pt Adobe Garamond Pro by Bookhouse, Sydney
Printed and bound in Australia by Griffin Press

10 9 8 7 6 5 4 3 2 1

The paper in this book is FSC® certified.
FSC® promotes environmentally responsible,
socially beneficial and economically viable
management of the world's forests.

Contents

Foreword

There are myriad publications celebrating the incomparable game of cricket and its players. However, rarely does a cricket book delve deeper into the underlying humanity of those players. Their strengths, weaknesses, philosophies, transgressions, motivational influences—in essence their character—is often passed over in the hurly-burly of documenting competitive play. Yet it is a player's character that ultimately determines the level of admiration from the fans.

In *Champions*, Mike Coward has skilfully extracted from the players the essential character required to be successful both on and off the field at the elite level. Reflective and insightful, Coward has teased out of each interviewee their personal and private stories.

In 2009, a unique oral-history project was commissioned by the Bradman Foundation, which operates the Bradman Museum and International Cricket Hall of Fame in Bowral, Australia. To collect, preserve and record the game's memory through interviews with Test players, umpires, journalists and world leaders was considered of paramount importance and a core educational resource for the International Cricket Hall of Fame.

Today's technology and its multiple platforms will ensure the game's global growth and impact on society are accessible through the Hall of Fame's portals, including its numerous museum galleries and mobile applications. To date the interview archive consists of over 130 of the world's foremost male and female Test cricketers together with other key personalities. All have freely contributed specifically for the benefit of young players and members of the public. As an educational tool, this book shows how cricket generates within players a sense of their own character, which ultimately delivers a deep love for the game and a passionate desire to respect and protect it.

The players universally provided their time generously and free of charge, regardless of their country of origin, because of the combined invitation from the Bradman Foundation and Mike Coward. *Champions* features selected extracts from the rich repository of interviews chosen by Mike Coward. The interviewees' generous gift begged to be shared in print.

I heartily commend it to the reader.

Richie Benaud OBE
Patron—Bradman Foundation

When considering the stature of an athlete, I place great store on certain qualities which I believe to be essential in addition to skill. They are that a person conducts his or her life with dignity, with integrity, with courage and perhaps most of all modesty. These virtues are totally compatible with pride, ambition, determination and competitiveness.

SIR DONALD BRADMAN, 1985

In the footsteps of the master: Australia's 43rd captain, Michael Clarke, pays his respects at the life-size statue of Sir Donald Bradman at the Bradman Museum and International Cricket Hall of Fame at Bowral.

CHAPTER ONE

Hail to the Hall of Fame

The Bradman International Cricket Hall of Fame at Bowral in the alluring southern highlands of New South Wales bears Sir Donald Bradman's name because he has been Australia's only universal cricketer.

Twelve years after his death at 92 in 2001 the legend of Bradman continues to thrive and while he railed against being perceived as a saintly figure, each year thousands of people visit the Hall of Fame to pay him homage and immerse themselves in the ancient and modern history of cricket.

As with the antecedent Bradman Museum, the Hall of Fame was inspired by Bradman's vision and continues to fulfil his wish that the game be 'honoured and strengthened' in his name.

While fate decreed his remarkable career as the greatest batsman was confined to Australia and England his time as an influential administrator and legislator saw the game grow exponentially beyond traditional boundaries.

Pre-eminent Australian and unabashed Anglophile, Bradman lived to see the game of Empire outlive the Empire and as both an emissary for the governors of the game in Australia and as a letter-writer nonpareil, he was in constant contact with cricket officials and devotees throughout the world.

The Hall of Fame was conceived in 2008 to mark the centenary of his birth and to recognise and celebrate the game's constant and dramatic evolution.

As with the Museum the international cricket hall exists to collect, preserve and exhibit the game's heritage and proudly trumpet its diversity of cultures and myriad languages. Furthermore, with the use of sophisticated technologies and the goodwill of the game's greatest cricketers, it provides the visitor with a memorable and entertaining interactive experience and a research resource without parallel.

In his introduction to *The Bradman Albums* in 1987, Bradman wrote:

> Inevitably the face of cricket changes with the passage of time. The game must adapt to the social era in which people live. Nobody, fifty years ago, could have foreshadowed night cricket, coloured clothing, white balls and so on, but I do not resile from such happenings provided we are able to preserve the underlying character-building edifice upon which the game was founded. This responsibility must be shouldered with care and

> foresight by contemporary players and administrators because they are now the custodians of a valued trust for future generations.

Bradman had unwavering belief in the spirit of cricket and challenged every cricket person to take responsibility for the welfare of the game and so safeguard its future. As a player he witnessed first-hand its welfare dangerously jeopardised during the white-hot Bodyline summer of 1932–33 and as an administrator saw the spirit imperilled at the height of the throwing controversies of the late 1950s and early 1960s. And as a trustee of the South Australian Cricket Association he was one of its delegates to the then Australian Cricket Board throughout the World Series Cricket schism from 1977 to 1979.

Financially supported by the Australian and New South Wales governments and built within metres of Bradman Oval and a renowned statue of the peerless batsman, the International Cricket Hall of Fame is the only exhibition of its kind in the burgeoning cricket world.

Notably it also provides the only formal presentation of the players inducted to the International Cricket Council's (ICC) Hall of Fame, which was established in 2009 in association with the Federation of International Cricketers' Associations to celebrate the centenary of the ICC.

And nearby spectacular silhouettes of the international hall's own 20 Greats of the Game invariably spark animated discussion. This elite group was chosen by a selection panel headed by Richie Benaud, the patron of the Bradman Foundation.

❖ ❖ ❖

The Bradman Foundation, a non-profit charitable trust, was established in 1987 with Bradman's wholehearted support. Its first initiatives were the establishment of the Museum and the Bradman Young Cricketer of the Year Award in 1989. Former Australian captain and International Cricket Hall of Fame ambassador Ricky Ponting is among a host of internationals who have won the award. Explosive opening batsman David Warner was honoured in 2012 and exciting Queenslander Joe Burns in 2013.

The Foundation is committed to youth development through cricket and each year organises coaching camps, hosts exhibition matches and events and offers university scholarships in Bradman's name.

The International Cricket Hall of Fame has brought a new and thrilling dimension to the Bradman precinct and the opening of the World Series Cricket exhibition during the 2012–13 season attracted widespread interest from visitors throughout Australia and overseas.

Recollections of World Series Cricket is the latest of the themed exhibitions which take the visitor from the rustic origins of the game by way of the extensive Bradman gallery to a high-tech presentation of today's vibrant and disparate cricket world.

The irony of Benaud serving as patron for an organisation bearing Bradman's name and loudly celebrating the World Series Cricket (WSC) revolution will not be lost on students of cricket history.

Arguably the two most progressive and influential thinkers in the annals of Australian cricket, they held strongly opposing views on World Series Cricket and did not speak for the two years the schism polarised the cricket community.

Benaud, Australia's 28th Test captain, was, with his wife and business partner Daphne, the leading cricket consultant to Kerry Packer throughout the tumultuous period.

Bradman, who was thought by many critics of the day to be conspicuously reluctant to speak publicly about the radical movement, at least privately remained steadfastly aligned with the game's traditional governors in vehement opposition to what they disparagingly called a 'circus'.

Benaud reflected on a long life in cricket and his role at the front line of the WSC uprising in his contribution to the Hall of Fame's interview archive. More than 130 of the game's foremost players, officials, writers, broadcasters and eminent enthusiasts from around the world have generously given their time to the project since it was commissioned in 2009.

I was delighted when Rina Hore, the executive director of the Foundation, charged me with the responsibility of coordinating the establishment of the archive.

After 40 years of writing about the game for various newspapers and magazines in Australia and overseas, it was a privilege to sit with the greatest players and officials of the past 70 years—a good number of whom I had known for many summers—to prompt their memories and reminiscences and seek their views on the major issues within the game.

With Sean Mulcahy, an outstanding cameraman with complementary audio, lighting and editing skills, I undertook the vast majority of the interviews and I will always be grateful for the spontaneity and honesty of the interviewees. The world's elite male and female cricketers readily acknowledged the need for a definitive archive and were deeply engaged in what will be an ongoing process.

The importance of conducting an interview when the opportunity arises was sombrely borne out between April 2010 and January 2013 with the death of five key figures whose memories had been recorded, transcribed and archived.

While Englishman Sir Alec Bedser was 91 and Australian Sam Loxton 90, Mansur Ali Khan Pataudi, the aristocratic former Indian captain was 70, English writer and broadcaster and former Marylebone Cricket Club president Christopher Martin-Jenkins, 67 and the South African-born internationalist, Tony Greig, 66. Martin-Jenkins left an exceptional body of work, and Greig, principally because of his decisive role in the World Series Cricket movement, will always be remembered as one of the most significant figures in the history of the game.

The interviews were conducted the length and breadth of Australia, in the Indian cities of Mumbai, New Delhi and Bangalore, at Potchefstroom in the North West Province of South Africa and Bridgetown, Barbados in the West Indies and in London, the home counties and midlands of England.

Such an extensive undertaking provided many logistical challenges and it was our good fortune that irrepressible Carlton Saldanha, a former first-class cricketer with Karnataka, used his considerable liaison and organisational skills to ease our brisk passage through India in 2010. The scorer of seven hundreds in a career which spanned 14 seasons and netted him 4066 runs at a healthy average of 45.68 before he turned his attention to operations and stadia rights acquisition for the Frontiers Group, his keenness and persuasiveness was as telling as his list of contacts.

He was on hand to ensure Sachin Tendulkar found his way from a meeting with sponsors to the interview in a sprawling function room at the palatial Taj Lands End Hotel at Bandra in Mumbai and ensured Kapil Dev could be intercepted during a business trip from Delhi to Mumbai.

Memories abound from this journey. Characteristically, Rahul Dravid honoured his commitment despite the pain of a jaw cracked in a hooking mishap during a Test match in Bangladesh a few days earlier, while Gundappa Viswanath, Erapalli Prasanna and Bhagwat Chandrasekhar prepared for their interview over chai and dosa on the clubhouse lawns of the Chinaswamy Stadium in Bangalore.

On cue, charismatic Bishan Bedi vented his spleen on contentious bowling actions before providing a fascinating insight into the arcane art of spin bowling and much more while holding court in a hotel basement in Delhi. Also in the nation's capital, Mansur Ali Khan Pataudi, in his elegant drawing room brimful of exquisite traditional and contemporary art and artefacts, in one of his last interviews spoke candidly of the unique challenges that face an Indian captain.

The journey to England and the West Indies the following year also was undertaken at pace and was particularly rewarding as news of the metamorphosis of the Bradman Museum and the establishment of the archive had preceded us.

We were based in a townhouse in Randolph Avenue, Maida Vale, which, with some imagination and a little help from the local florist, could be converted to a suitable space for filming. Ten of the 21 interviewees slated for England welcomed the convenient location in London, some happily taking a constitutional stroll from nearby Lord's cricket ground to fulfil their commitment.

There were, too, journeys to the country to capture some of the quarry. Certainly it was something of a coup to ambush former England captain Ted Dexter at his beloved Sunningdale Golf Club in Berkshire during a visit from his home in Nice on the French Riviera. Kept off the course by a recurring back complaint, he reflected and reminisced in a sumptuous lounge of the clubhouse, its walls lined with photographs of peerless golfers.

John Snow, one of the greatest of all fast bowlers, was so preoccupied with preparations for a daughter's wedding he momentarily forgot the arrangement at the Sussex County ground at Hove. However, he soon recovered ground and characteristically, if metaphorically, pushed off his long run.

Visits to renowned writers John Woodcock at Longparish in Hampshire and David Frith at Guildford in Surrey were followed by splendid lunches at homely village pubs before thoughts turned to more hours at the wheel to reach Ray Illingworth and Rohan Kanhai in the north of the country.

Illingworth, who famously regained the Ashes for England in Australia in 1970–71, was regaining strength at his home in Farnley, Yorkshire, after a long hospitalisation following a heart attack. But it was evident soon enough he had lost none of his toughness and, as ever, did not mince his words.

Kanhai, the former West Indian captain who so boldly took the Wisden Trophy from Illingworth in a three-Test series in England in 1973, has long lived at Poulton in Lancashire and he too was finding his strength after a worrying bronchial illness. The opportunity to relive the halcyon days of West Indian cricket under Frank Worrell soon brought a smile to his face and a lilt to his voice.

The stimulating time with Kanhai whetted the appetite for the trip to Barbados for a clutch of interviews and a pilgrimage to the grave of Worrell at the Barbados campus of the University of the West Indies at Cave Hill, a few minutes' drive north of Bridgetown.

And not even the challenges posed by extensive renovations undertaken at the Coral Mist resort during filming took the gloss from the exercise. The learned and loved voice of West Indian cricket, Tony Cozier, along with peerless Wes Hall and champions from the 1980s, provided a special perspective of the game that unites the disparate sovereign nations of the vast Caribbean Archipelago.

While some interviews within Australia were coordinated at the International Hall of Fame, the Cricket Australia Centre of Excellence in Brisbane and at various Test match venues, others were conducted privately.

That so many of the game's most recognisable identities so willingly opened the doors of their homes was indicative of the importance all subjects placed on the faithful recollection of the past to inform and benefit future generations. For many it was a priceless and perhaps final opportunity to make a telling, defining or clarifying observation for posterity.

The following pages contain extracts from some of the interviews distilled into categories that historically resonated with Bradman: leadership, courage, philosophy, the spirit of the game and humour and hubris.

The World of Cricket gallery provides visitors to the International Cricket Hall of Fame with a rare opportunity to explore the remarkable reach of the game which was once seen as a curiosity of the British Empire. And a deft movement of a hand at the interactive touch table in front of the map of cricket's New World is sufficient to yield priceless information about the 106 countries which comprise the International Cricket Council in 2013.

Australian captain Mark Taylor (left) and his English counterpart Mike Atherton wear more than their heart on their sleeve. Brave opening batsmen, they matched wits as opposing captains in 11 Ashes Tests in the mid 1990s.

CHAPTER TWO

The cast

The cast of 58 cricketers assembled for *Champions* is beyond compare.

Testament to the stature of the men and women who enliven the following pages in such an eloquent and entertaining manner is that 37 of them captained their country in Test matches.

That there are five knights and a baroness among them adds further lustre.

These gifted and giving denizens of the cricket world, aged from 32 to 91, hail from 14 countries—including Italy and Zambia—and with disarming honesty share their deepest thoughts on the glorious game.

JONATHAN AGNEW

born Macclesfield, Cheshire, England
4 April 1960

'Aggers', as he is known to his myriad admirers, is the cricket correspondent for the British Broadcasting Corporation and has also written on the game. Renowned for his affability and sense of fun, he is philosophical that many of his worldwide audience are oblivious to the fact he had a fine career as a fast bowler for Leicestershire and played three Test matches for England in the mid 1980s. He took 666 first-class wickets at 29.25 between 1978 and 1990. 'Aggers' fell in love with cricket commentary as a boy on the family farm, and as a broadcaster was guided by the doyen, Richie Benaud.

WASIM AKRAM

born Lahore, Pakistan
3 June 1966

Akram is considered by many pundits to be the greatest left-arm fast bowler of all time. Mentored by the legendary Javed Miandad and Imran Khan, whose photographs adorned his bedroom wall as a youth, Akram was an artist who mastered every aspect of fast seam and swing bowling. The very best batsmen of his era believe he made the ball talk. Also an explosive if under-achieving batsman at Test level, his reputation lost some lustre during the match-fixing controversies of the 1990s. He captured 414 Test wickets at 23.62 in 102 Test matches and 502 wickets at 23.52 in limited-over internationals and captained Pakistan in 25 Tests between 1993 and 1999.

MIKE ATHERTON

born Manchester, Lancashire, England
23 March 1968

Courageous and unbending, Atherton always displayed the stoicism for which the English cricketer is traditionally renowned. A self-disciplined and highly motivated opening batsman, he possessed exceptional patience and powers of concentration. This was never more evident than in Johannesburg in 1996 when he defied a South African attack headed by Alan Donald and Shaun Pollock for 10 hours and 43 minutes for a defining unconquered 185 to save England from defeat. Critics pondered whether it was the finest match-saving innings by an England captain. Given the leadership at the age of 25 when stocks were low and victory elusive he enjoyed series successes against South Africa and the West Indies. He famously struggled against Australia or, more pointedly, Glenn McGrath, who dismissed him on a world-record 19 occasions.

Given he was plagued by a serious back complaint throughout his career, Atherton showed remarkable resilience by playing 115 Test matches over 12 years from 1989 for 7728 runs at 37.69 with 16 centuries. Following his retirement in 2001 he seamlessly joined the ranks of the Fourth Estate and soon became one of the most accomplished writers and broadcasters in the game.

BISHAN BEDI

born Amritsar, Punjab, India
25 September 1946

Wearing trademark patkas of vibrant colours, 'Bish' was a much-loved orthodox slow left-arm bowler who bewitched batsmen with his loop and subtle variations of pace, dip and angle. Along with Erapalli Prasanna, Bhagwat Chandrasekhar and Srinivas Venkataraghavan he formed a quartet of slow bowlers who enthralled and entertained crowds the world over throughout the 1960s and 1970s. India's 19th captain, Bedi took 266 Test match wickets at 28.71 and a colossal 1560 at 21.69 in a first-class career from 1961 to 1981. Passionate about the development of young cricketers, he remains a forthright critic intent on preserving the traditional values of the game.

RICHIE BENAUD

born Penrith, New South Wales, Australia
6 October 1930

Australia's 28th Test captain, Benaud suffered only four defeats in 27 Tests as captain and never lost a series. A leg-spinner with considerable ability as a batsman as three Test hundreds attest, he and West Indian contemporary Frank Worrell are credited with reviving Test cricket from its moribund state in 1960–61. Renowned for engineering a remarkable victory against England by bowling around the wicket at Old Trafford in 1961, Benaud was a key figure in the revolutionary World Series Cricket movement in the 1970s. A strong advocate of players' rights, Benaud, into his eighties remains the game's pre-eminent analyst and critic.

ALLAN BORDER

born Cremorne, New South Wales, Australia
27 July 1955

AB, as he is always and affectionately known, has some entitlement to be regarded as Australia's greatest cricketer after Sir Donald Bradman. When he retired in 1994 as Test cricket's highest run-scorer (11,174) he had used his indomitable spirit to single-handedly revive the fortunes of Australian cricket. A cricketer's cricketer and indisputably the people's cricketer, 153 of his 156 Tests were played consecutively, 93 as captain. Flint-hard, courageous and resilient, he evolved into an enterprising captain after a 4–0 Ashes triumph in England in 1989. Two years earlier he had held the World Cup aloft in India. His occasional contrariness, which led to the harsh sobriquet of 'Captain Grumpy', was forgiven by a grateful sporting nation.

SIR IAN BOTHAM

born Oldfield, Cheshire, England
24 November 1955

Universally known as 'Beefy', Botham was a force of nature—an indestructible, incorrigible, incomparable all-rounder of remarkable talent, strength and stamina. Fastest to the imposing double of 1000 runs and 100 wickets, he was not only England's most celebrated cricketer of his time but the country's pre-eminent and controversial sporting personality. Devoid of self-doubt, he intimidated and imposed himself on every contest. In 1981 and despite the loss of the captaincy, he changed the course of a series with Australia now familiarly known as 'Botham's Ashes'. During his career, he achieved the remarkable feat of scoring a century and claiming five or more wickets in an innings five times. He took 200 Test wickets by age 25; overall he netted 383 wickets at 28.40 and scored 5200 runs at 33.54 with 14 hundreds. His long-distance walks raised millions of dollars for charity.

MIKE BREARLEY

born Harrow, Middlesex, England
28 April 1942

Despite a modest record as a Test batsman (1442 runs at 22.88), Brearley was one of England's greatest and most cerebral captains. Renowned for his people and communication skills, he led in 31 of his 39 Tests and won 18 matches and lost only four. A psychoanalyst by profession, Brearley's acclaimed book, *The Art of Captaincy*, is a respected reference text in realms well beyond cricket. Fascinated by the tactical and strategic aspects of the game from his youth, his lack of intellectual snobbery and friendliness were said by his peers to be significant qualities. The Australian fast bowler Rodney Hogg famously observed that Brearley 'had a degree in people'. Brearley led England from 1977 to 1981 when the game was split asunder by the World Series Cricket upheaval.

GREG CHAPPELL

born Unley, South Australia
7 August 1948

The second of three renowned cricketing brothers, Greg Chappell was among the most poised and elegant of batsmen. Upright at the crease and an instinctive and imperious stroke player, he was also a most useful medium-pace bowler and a brilliant fieldsman. He bookended his 87-Test career with centuries and retired to diverse business interests and later international cricket coaching with 7110 runs at an imposing average of 53.86. He succeeded his older brother Ian as Australian captain and was at the helm in England in 1977 when the international cricket community learned of the polarising World Series Cricket movement. Physically and mentally exhausted by the increased demands of the captaincy, he conceded he was not fit to be in the job when he ordered his brother Trevor to bowl underarm against New Zealand in 1981. It is his one regret in a glittering career.

IAN CHAPPELL

born Unley, South Australia
26 September 1943

Thirty-five years after his grandfather Vic Richardson led Australia, Ian Chappell was appointed his country's 34th captain. 'Never captain like a Victorian', was Richardson's provocative if oblique advice. The imagination and boldness that would characterise Chappell's leadership was evident from his first match when he invited England to bat. He led on 30 occasions and never lost a series. Renowned for his pride, honesty and fierce loyalty to his charges, Chappelli was not blessed with the style of his brother Greg but was a strong, resourceful and courageous batsman at three, given to hooking and pulling. The cricketer many a soul would choose to bat for their life, he was also a brilliant slips fieldsman and occasional leg-spinner. Defiant and unbending by nature, he was often in conflict with the game's establishment and was in the vanguard of the World Series Cricket movement.

ALAN DAVIDSON

born Gosford, New South Wales, Australia
14 June 1929

For 50 years Australian cricket has searched in vain for a fast bowler of Davidson's class and ability to score significant runs from number eight. An intelligent left-arm paceman operating smoothly from 15 paces, Davidson was also a highly accomplished fieldsman and dubbed 'The Claw' because of his brilliance in the gully. His performance in the historic tied Test match with the West Indies at Brisbane in December 1960 is a part of the rich lore of Australian cricket. Ignoring the discomfort of a broken finger, he became the first player to complete the match double of 100 runs (44 and 80) and 10 wickets (11–222) and in all probability would have guided Australia to a famous victory had he not been dramatically run out by Richie Benaud. He captured 186 wickets at a miserly 20.53 in 44 Tests and in retirement presided over Cricket NSW for a record 33 years.

TED DEXTER

born Milan, Italy

15 May 1935

Inevitably given his aristocratic air, Dexter, a debonair Cambridge blue, was universally known as Lord Ted or Lord Edward. A handsome adventurer and gifted all-round sportsman, he was a fearless and powerful batsman who relished counter-attacking the fastest bowling. A daring 70 against West Indians Wes Hall and Charlie Griffith at Lord's in 1963 is a precious part of English cricket lore. Although he sometimes unsettled the hierarchy by practising golf shots in the field, he captained England on 30 occasions from 1961. He scored 4502 runs at 47.89 with nine centuries but too often was required to save rather than win a Test match. He also bowled at a lively medium pace. Dexter continued to serve the game in administrative roles and with Colin Cowdrey was responsible for the drafting of the 2000 'Spirit of Cricket' preamble to the laws of the game.

MS (Mahendra Singh) DHONI

born Ranchi, Jharkhand, India
7 July 1981

The meteoric rise of MS Dhoni to a position of influence and great wealth in cricket's richest and most powerful jurisdiction is a story for the ages. From cricket's backlands in the mining state of Jharkhand, at 22 he worked as a ticket collector and occasional platform announcer for the Indian Railways outside Kolkata. At 23 he began his remarkable international career in a one-day international against Bangladesh and a year later took his home-spun philosophy and style of batting and wicketkeeping into the Test match arena. A pragmatic and proud representative of the new and burgeoning Indian middle-class, at 26 he captained India to victory in the inaugural World Twenty and instantly became a hero to India's cricket-crazed masses. Promotion to the leadership in the one-day international and Test match arenas followed and he also had the distinction of gaining India the number one Test ranking for 18 months from December 2009 and engineered a famous victory in the 50-over World Cup in 2011. By 2013 when he became the first captain to lead India to four wins in a series (against Australia) he rivalled Sachin Tendulkar for fame and fortune.

RAHUL DRAVID

born Indore, Madhya Pradesh, India
11 January 1973

Known as 'The Wall' because of his impenetrable defence and the value he attached to his wicket, Dravid bestrode the Test arena for 16 years as India evolved into the most influential force in world cricket. Batting at three ahead of Sachin Tendulkar, he amassed 13,288 runs at 52.31 with 36 centuries in 164 Test matches. Essentially a classicist, he was resilient and resourceful enough to play with great success in the shorter forms of the game and for the sake of team balance often kept wicket in the 50-over game. Greatly respected and admired by his contemporaries, he was a brilliant slips fieldsman and holds the record for the most number of catches in Test matches. The most genial of men, he was a much decorated player and at the end of his career had the honour of delivering the Bradman oration at the Australian War Memorial in Canberra.

JOEL GARNER

born Christ Church, Barbados
16 December 1952

A monolithic paceman with perhaps the most lethal yorker the game has seen, Garner was a member of the famed phalanx of fast bowlers who were irresistible at Clive Lloyd's direction in the 1980s. Standing at 203.2 cm 'Big Bird', as he was universally known, terrorised batsmen with the yorker—perfected as a youth by bowling endlessly at a solitary stump—and the wicked lift he gained from barely short of a good length. An affable, smiling soul much loved wherever the West Indies played, Garner captured 259 wickets at a miserly 20.97. Of the game's leading wicket-takers only his Bajan compatriot and regular new ball partner and friend Malcolm Marshall (20.94) was fractionally more economical. That he took five wickets in an innings on only seven occasions is evidence enough of the extraordinary depth of the West Indies bowling at that time. He was just as parsimonious in 98 one-day internationals, his 146 wickets coming at 18.84. He claimed 5–38 to devastate England in the 1979 World Cup final at Lord's.

SUNIL GAVASKAR

born Bombay (Mumbai), Maharashtra, India
10 July 1949

Standing 5 ft 5 in (165 cm) and so fractionally shorter than Don Bradman, Sunny was one of the greatest of all opening batsmen. Compact and calm he honed a flawless technique and an ability to concentrate unerringly over long periods. He gave immediate notice of his genius, amassing 774 runs at a phenomenal average of 154.80 against the West Indies in his first four Tests at the age of 21. By dint of his discipline and determination he instilled a sorely needed professionalism to the elite of Indian cricket and was awarded the captaincy on 47 occasions between 1976 and 1985. Gavaskar broke records throughout his career and was the first player to eclipse Bradman's record of 29 Test centuries and to reach 10,000 Test match runs. He compiled 10,122 runs at 51.12 with 34 centuries in 125 Test matches. Since 1996 Australia and India have played for the Border–Gavaskar Trophy.

ADAM GILCHRIST

born Bellingen, New South Wales, Australia
14 November 1971

Espousing the simplest but most thrilling batting philosophy, Gilchrist was the most exhilarating player in the world at the start of the 21st century. 'Just hit the ball' was his credo and he was universally loved because of it. Whether batting at seven in the Test arena or opening in the short forms, he brought crowds to the game. He scored 5570 Test runs at 47.60 with a strike rate of 81.95 and 9619 runs at 35.89 runs and a strike rate of 96.94 in one-day internationals. Such were his freakish batting feats—notably his 57-ball Ashes hundred in Perth in 2006–07—that his considerable accomplishments as a wicketkeeper were sometimes unrecognised. He developed into a fine gloveman and completed 905 international dismissals. Australia's 41st captain and conqueror of the 'Final Frontier' in India in 2004, he was, briefly, statistically the leading 'keeper in Test cricket.

DAVID GOWER

born Tunbridge Wells, Kent, England
1 April 1957

One of the most aesthetically pleasing batsmen of any era, spectators of all ages demanded to see Gower despite the fact he would exasperate as often as he would enthral. Tall and still at the crease, this left-hander with a shock of fair curly hair was an exquisite timer of the ball and, until his shoulder gave way disabling his throwing arm, one of the world's most skilled and exciting fieldsmen. Such was his natural brilliance much was always expected of him and lapses in form invariably were ascribed to carelessness and an inability to concentrate. At his peak he had no peer. He played innings of genuine significance in Pakistan, India, West Indies and Australia and in the 1985 Ashes series gathered 732 runs at an average of 81.33, a new record for a home series with Australia. He had the misfortune as captain to regularly confront the incomparable West Indian teams of the 1980s. He retired in 1992 after 117 Tests (8231 runs at 44.25) and turned immediately and with characteristic effortlessness to a prosperous career as a television commentator, presenter and entertainer.

TONY GREIG

born Queenstown, Cape Province, South Africa
6 October 1946

There has been no more dramatic and controversial figure in contemporary cricket than this internationalist. Born of a Scottish father and an English–South African mother in the iniquitous old South Africa, Greig captained England before aligning himself with World Series Cricket and moving to Australia, where he remained in the employ of Kerry Packer. Extroverted and blessed with considerable all-round skills, he imposed himself on opposition and could change the course of a match with his bold rough-hewn stroke play or his bouncy, aggressive fast-medium or fast off-spin bowling. Also a brilliant slipper he averaged considerably more in Test cricket (40.43) than the first-class arena (31.19), which underscored both his undisguised intent and innate combativeness. He complemented his 3599 Test runs with 141 wickets at 32.30. A strategically savvy captain, on occasions he was impetuous and intemperate and paid dearly for his infamous 'grovel' comment before the West Indies 1976 tour of England. Greig suffered a heart attack and died on 29 December 2012 aged 66.

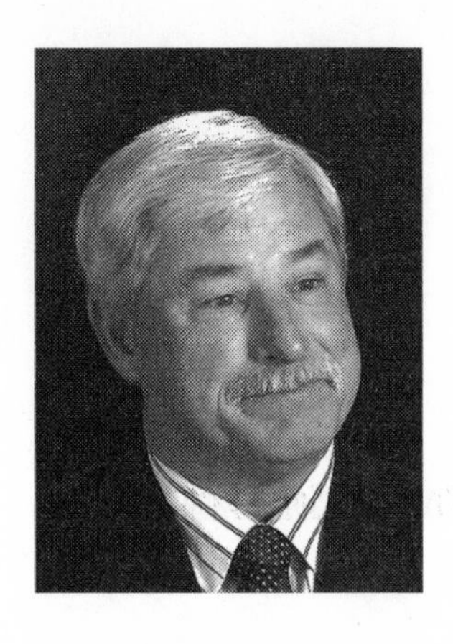

SIR RICHARD HADLEE

born Christchurch, New Zealand
3 July 1951

The consummate professional whose attention to detail knew no bounds, Hadlee carried the fortunes of New Zealand cricket throughout his remarkable 17-year international career. One of the most intelligent of all fast bowlers, he took a staggering 34.34 per cent of his country's wickets. Such responsibility took its toll and he was one of the first elite cricketers to speak publicly of depression. Renowned as much for his single-mindedness as his guile, he was the first bowler to take 400 wickets in Tests and retired with 431 wickets at the startling average of 22.29. Nine times he took 10 or more wickets in a match, including 15–123 against Australia at Brisbane in 1985–86. He also scored two Test hundreds and was considered one of the four great all-rounders of the 1980s along with Ian Botham, Imran Khan and Kapil Dev.

SIR WES HALL

born Station Hill, St Michael, Barbados
12 September 1937

One of the most charismatic and loved of all cricketers, Hall was among the fastest of bowlers and put the fear of God into batsmen the world over for a decade from the late 1950s. Operating from an intimidatingly long run and with a gold crucifix thumping against his torso, he made a thrilling spectacle as he spearheaded the West Indies attack for his captain, muse and protector, Frank Worrell. Summoned by the selectors for a tour of India and Pakistan in 1958–59 he took 46 wickets in eight Test matches to quickly establish an impressive reputation. In the tied Test at Brisbane in December 1960 he captured 9–203 from 47.2 overs and famously bowled the sensational final over. An incomparable raconteur, his account of this final over is a precious part of the game's mythology. He claimed 192 wickets at an average of 26.38 in 48 Tests before retiring to life as a cricket administrator and manager, an influential minister in the Barbados government and an ordained minister in the service of his God.

NEIL HARVEY

born Fitzroy, Victoria, Australia
8 October 1928

Forever known as the 'baby' of Don Bradman's 1948 undefeated Invincibles tour of England, Harvey was a richly talented left-handed batsman and an exceptional fieldsman. Quick on his feet and a thrilling and precise stroke player he won a legion of followers from his second appearance—against India, at Melbourne—when at 19 years and 121 days he became the youngest Australian to score a Test century. International recognition followed when he gathered 112 in the celebrated Headingley Test of 1948 and he tallied six hundreds in his first 13 Test innings. In South Africa in 1949–50 he amassed 660 runs at 132.00 with four hundreds in five Tests. A fiercely loyal vice-captain to Richie Benaud from 1958–59 on, he ended his 15-year career with 6149 runs at 48.41 with 21 centuries and continued to serve the game as a national selector for 12 years. Often an outspoken critic of the contemporary game and the technique of its practitioners, he was inducted into the Australian Cricket Hall of Fame in 2000.

MATTHEW HAYDEN

born Kingaroy, Queensland, Australia
29 October 1971

Immensely powerful of mind and body, Hayden retired as statistically Australia's greatest opening batsman. After a faltering start when his technique was loudly questioned, he amassed 8625 runs at 50.73 from 103 Tests with 30 centuries. An intimidator respected and feared in equal measure by bowlers and fieldsmen everywhere, he scored 1000 or more runs in five consecutive years from 2001. He amassed 380 against Zimbabwe in 2003–04 when he briefly borrowed from Brian Lara the record for the highest score in Test matches. Fearless and audacious he established with Justin Langer one of the most productive and celebrated of all opening combinations. At his zenith he joined Don Bradman and England's Ken Barrington as the only men to score hundreds in four consecutive Tests. Hayden was also an accomplished limited-over player and a member of two World Cup–winning teams.

BARONESS RACHAEL HEYHOE-FLINT

born Wolverhampton, England
11 June 1939

One of the first 10 women admitted to the Marylebone Cricket Club (MCC) as members in 1999, the name Heyhoe-Flint is synonymous with women's cricket the world over. England captain for 12 years and unbeaten in six series from 1966, her initiative and influence was responsible for the first women's World Cup in 1973 two years before the men. An outstanding batter, she scored 1594 runs at 45.54 in 22 Test matches and averaged an impressive 58.45 in 23 limited-overs matches. At the age of 37 she batted for just shy of nine hours for 179 to save England from a Test defeat against Australia at The Oval. A charismatic woman and an accomplished public speaker, she further enhanced the profile of women's cricket when she became the first woman elected to the full MCC committee in 2004. The first woman inducted to the International Cricket Hall of Fame (ICC), she had the privilege of leading the first women's team to play at Lord's.

MICHAEL HOLDING

born Kingston, Jamaica
16 February 1954

That he wore the epithet 'Whispering Death' is evidence enough of the threat Michael Holding posed to batsmen the world over. Tall, lissom and athletic, he was the most majestic of bowlers and his 249 wickets came at 23.68 in 60 Test matches. He was a member of a posse of intimidating fast bowlers Clive Lloyd summoned to enforce the West Indies' superiority throughout the 1980s. Like many of his generation he was carefully mentored by Lloyd and without question followed him into the breakaway World Series Cricket movement where his reputation was forged. At one time vice-captain to Viv Richards, Holding was a proud and passionate competitor whose innocence as a cricketer was shattered on his first tour of Australia in 1975 at the age of 21 when he was wrongly denied the critical wicket of Ian Chappell in Sydney. In retirement Holding became one of the most outspoken and insightful of television cricket commentators and in demand the world over.

MICHAEL HUSSEY

born Perth, Western Australia
27 May 1975

A relentless accumulator of runs with infinite patience and exceptional powers of concentration, Hussey was six months into his 31st year before he was chosen for his first Test match in 2005. The long wait in the wings fired his imagination and ambition and he became the fastest player to score 1000 Test runs. After two years in the Test team his average was a staggering 86.18 and he was the talk of the international cricket community. The nous and experience gained during a long apprenticeship in Sheffield Shield and County cricket served him well and he became known for his persistence and reliability. To his unease these qualities led to his sobriquet 'Mr Cricket'. Proud and self-disciplined he captained Australia in limited-over cricket and has also proven adept and successful in the Twenty20 format.

RAY ILLINGWORTH

born Pudsey, Yorkshire, England
8 June 1932

A hard-headed all-rounder, Illingworth was a more accomplished cricketer than a cursory glance at his Test statistics might suggest. He was a natural and outstanding leader of men who had the distinction of regaining the Ashes in Australia in 1970–71. Hailing from the birthplace of his hero, legendary Sir Leonard Hutton, his exceptional skills as a tactician and strategist became widely known when at 36 and in high dudgeon he left his beloved Yorkshire to captain Leicestershire. Within two years and after Colin Cowdrey had torn his left Achilles tendon, Illingworth began his 31-Test career as England captain. An intimate knowledge of opponents' capacities, combined with the canniest of field placements, made him the stingiest of off-spinners. Unerringly accurate he conceded 1.91 runs per over while taking 122 wickets at 31.20 in his 61 Test matches over a 15-year career from 1958. He also scored two Test hundreds and had the distinction of playing against Don Bradman, who came out of retirement (for five deliveries, as it happened) to play for Prime Minister Robert Menzies' XI against the English tourists in February 1963.

MAHELA JAYAWARDENE

born Colombo, Sri Lanka
27 May 1977

Blessed with an abundance of natural talent, Jayawardene was the first Sri Lankan batsman to reach 10,000 Test runs. And for good measure he has also scored more than 10,000 runs in limited-over internationals. Also one of the great slips fieldsmen of his generation, he shares with his dear friend Kumar Sangakkara the capacity to occupy the crease for long periods. Indeed, the first of the double hundreds for which they are both renowned, came in just his seventh Test match in 1999. In 2006 the pair pooled their priceless resources and added a record 624 for the third wicket against South Africa. Jayawardene's contribution of 374 is the fourth-highest individual score in history. An affable man who has endeavoured to distance himself from the complex and often confronting politics of Sri Lankan cricket, Jayawardene has had successful periods as captain and was at the helm when Sri Lanka reached the World Cup final in 2007.

KAPIL DEV

born Chandigarh, Punjab, India
6 January 1959

If becoming India's greatest paceman and fast-bowling all-rounder did not assure Kapil Dev of immortality in India, engineering the shock defeat of the West Indies in the 1983 World Cup final surely did. India was instantly seduced by the compressed game and never fully regained its regard for Test cricket. Despite being reared on pitches that traditionally broke the heart and often the back of the fast men, Kapil Dev toiled off his long run for 16 years and eventually took from Richard Hadlee the record for the aggregate of Test wickets. He finished with 434 wickets at 29.64. He complemented this accomplishment with 5248 runs at 31.05 with eight centuries—one so memorably in the tied Test match with Australia at Chennai in 1986. An uncomplicated cricketer of considerable flair, in 2002 he was voted India's Cricketer of the 20th Century ahead of Sunil Gavaskar and Sachin Tendulkar.

ANIL KUMBLE

born Bangalore, Karnataka, India
17 October 1970

Evoking memories of Bill O'Reilly and Bhagwat Chandrasekhar, indefatigable Kumble bowled his fast leg breaks and cutters with unerring accuracy and menacing bounce. A modest, earnest and proud professional, he plied his trade for 18 years and finished his 132-Test career with 619 wickets (at 29.65) behind only fellow spinners Muttiah Muralitharan and Shane Warne. A protégé of Chandrasekhar, he was devastating on wearing pitches especially in India and was just as effective in the 50-over game where he claimed 337 wickets at 30.89. He was feted throughout the cricket world in 1998–99 when he became the only bowler aside from Englishman Jim Laker in 1956 to take all 10 wickets in an innings—10–74 against Pakistan at Delhi. He had just entered his 38th year when appointed India's 30th captain. He engineered India's first home success against Pakistan in 27 years before revealing impressive managerial and diplomatic skills during a controversial series in Australia in 2007–08.

BRIAN LARA

born Cantaro, Santa Cruz, Trinidad
2 May 1969

The one constant of West Indian cricket at the close of the 20th century and into the new millennium was the presumption that Lara would always meet the every expectation of a demanding archipelago. At times such conjecture inspired him and his run-scoring was phenomenal. At other times he was overwhelmed and defeated and he polarised opinion especially when entrusted with the captaincy. On song the prodigiously talented, diminutive left-hander dazzled with his thrilling and daring stroke play and his capacity to construct massive scores. The international cricket community was agog in 1994 when in the space of two months he compiled innings of 375 and 501 not out to break the world record for the highest Test and first-class scores. This peak was followed by a trough until a remarkable revival against Australia in 1998–99. And so the pattern continued. He retired with 11,953 runs at 52.88 with 34 centuries—nine of them being doubles. Only Bradman scored more double centuries.

BILL LAWRY

born Thornbury, Victoria, Australia
11 February 1937

The butt of much humour because of his pronounced nose and a conservative approach to batting and captaincy, Lawry was a fine and courageous batsman who joined forces with Bob Simpson to form one of the most formidable of all opening partnerships. In Barbados in 1964–65 they added 382 against a West Indian attack comprising Wes Hall, Charlie Griffith, Garry Sobers and Lance Gibbs. A tall angular figure, Lawry earned rave reviews on his first tour to England in 1961 when in just his second Test he boldly withstood a barrage from Fred Trueman and Brian Statham on the infamous Lord's Ridge and scored the first of his 13 centuries. Over the next decade he scored 5234 runs at 47.15. He possessed infinite patience and in consecutive years at the end of the 1960s carried his bat against India and England. His outspokenness after an ill-conceived visit to South Africa was appended to the Indian tour of 1969–70 cost him the captaincy and possibly a fourth England trip in 1972.

DENNIS LILLEE

born Subiaco, Western Australia
18 July 1949

In the minds of many judges the greatest fast bowler of them all, Lillee overcame shocking spinal stress fractures to take his place in the pantheon. In full cry this charismatic champion made a great spectacle, crowds ritually chanting his name at every stride. Combative and intensely competitive by nature, he exploded into the consciousness of the international cricket fraternity when he captured 8–29 against a glittering World XI in Perth in 1971. In the mid 1970s he joined forces with Jeff Thomson and together they intimidated with their frightening pace and routed England and the West Indies. Challenging to captain he was periodically involved in controversy—most notably for a contretemps with legendary and provocative Pakistani Javed Miandad and an ill-fated attempt to bring an aluminium bat to the world stage. He broke Lance Gibbs's world record of 309 Test wickets, finished with 355 wickets at 23.92 and was the key driver of the World Series Cricket movement.

CLIVE LLOYD

born Georgetown, British Guiana (now Guyana)
31 August 1944

With Sir Frank Worrell his exemplar, tall, languid Lloyd used communication and diplomatic skills to band together as brothers the cricketers from the disparate sovereign nations which comprise the vast Caribbean archipelago. Under his leadership the West Indies became the most powerful force in world cricket and set the standard for 20 years to the mid 1990s. A bespectacled left-hander who used a heavy bat with devastating effect, his reaction to the 5–1 defeat to Australia at the hands of fast bowlers Dennis Lillee and Jeff Thomson in 1975–76 changed the course of the modern game. Dismissing accusations of intimidatory bowling and tediously slow over-rates, Lloyd called upon a bevy of great fast bowlers to ensure the invincibility of his team. He won 36 and lost 12 of his 74 Tests at the helm and was the first West Indian player to earn 100 Test caps. The scorer of 7515 Test runs at 46.67, he led the West Indies to victory in the first two World Cups in 1975 and 1979.

RICK McCOSKER

born Inverell, New South Wales, Australia
11 December 1946

A tall, poised opening batsman, McCosker is numbered among the many fine Test cricketers to have emerged from the New South Wales country. Four consecutive Sheffield Shield centuries earned him selection for the final three Test matches of the 1974–75 Ashes series at age 28. An impressive 80 on debut saw him chosen for the 1975 tour of England where he topped the averages with 414 runs at 82.80, including a century at The Oval. At Headingley, Leeds, he was undefeated on 95 when the match was abandoned after vandals sabotaged the pitch in the early hours of the fifth day. He also played in each match of Australia's first World Cup campaign. McCosker is well remembered for the courage he showed to bat with a broken jaw in a decisive partnership with century-scorer Rod Marsh in the Centenary Test of 1977. He returned briefly to Test cricket after joining World Series Cricket.

GLENN McGRATH

born Dubbo, New South Wales, Australia
9 February 1970

Statistically, McGrath is the most miserly of Australia's pre-eminent bowlers. The world's leading wicket-taker among fast bowlers, his 563 wickets came at 21.64. Of all-comers only the West Indian triumvirate of Malcolm Marshall, Joel Garner and Curtly Ambrose and England's Fred Trueman have been fractionally stingier. McGrath was sharp but not a fast bowler in the true sense. His skill was his unerring, relentless off-stump accuracy, subtle variations of pace and nasty bounce. To the occasional unease of his captain he often publicly targeted particular opponents. In the case of England opener Mike Atherton and West Indian maestro Brian Lara in particular, it was a stunningly successful tactic. The first fast bowler to play 100 Tests for Australia, he was also an outstanding bowler in the limited-over arena and enjoyed great success in the World Cup triumphs of 2003 and 2007.

GRAHAM McKENZIE

born Perth, Western Australia
24 June 1941

Named Garth after the immensely strong comic strip hero of the time, McKenzie had an impressive physique and a magnificent action for a fast bowler, based in part on the silky style of the great Ray Lindwall. Deceptively quick, he made an immediate impact when chosen as a teenager to tour England in 1961 and took the first of his 16 hauls of five or more wickets in an innings in his Test debut at Lord's a fortnight after his 20th birthday. Always poised and unassuming, he had completed 100 wickets by the age of 23 and 200 by 27. However, in time, overwork took a dreadful physical and mental toll and more than anyone he was a victim of the administrative folly of affixing a four-Test tour of South Africa to a full five-Test tour of India in 1969–70. As shabbily treated as his captain Bill Lawry, in 1970–71, he left for a life as a professional with Leicestershire with 246 wickets at 29.78—two shy of the then Australian record held by Richie Benaud.

ARTHUR MORRIS

born Bondi, New South Wales, Australia
19 January 1922

The most gracious of men and elegant of left-handers, Morris declared his brilliance when three weeks before his 19th birthday he used a bat borrowed from the club kit at St George in Sydney to be the first cricketer anywhere to score a century in each innings of his first first-class match. Only India's Nari Contractor (1952–53) and Pakistan's Aamer Malik (1979–80) have emulated the achievement. He also scored centuries in his initial first-class appearances in England, South Africa and the West Indies—a feat not yet equalled. Named alongside Bill Ponsford in the Australian team of the 20th century, he twice captained Australia. He compiled 3533 runs at 46.48 in 46 Tests between November 1946 and June 1955, and with 696 runs at 87.00, famously outscored even Don Bradman in the five Tests of the 1948 Invincibles tour of England.

MUTTIAH MURALITHARAN

born Kandy, Sri Lanka
17 April 1972

Known both as champion and cheat this unique spinner divided the cricket community like no other since England captain Douglas Jardine cocked a snook and doffed his Harlequin cap to irate Australian crowds in 1932–33. His most strident critics consider he is responsible for changes to the laws that legitimise throwing. Taunted and tormented by detractors everywhere after being twice called for bowling with an illegal action in Australia in 1995 and 1999, for a time he was asked not to bowl his renowned doosra as it exceeded the 15-degree tolerance measure. Supple of wrist and a prodigious turner of the ball, he was proud and competitive by nature and somehow maintained a sunny disposition and wide-eyed smile. He prospered at a time dominated by the exploits of a plethora of high-class slow bowlers to become the highest wicket-taker in both Test and limited-over international (LOI) cricket. His 800 Test wickets came at 22.72 from 133 matches and his 534 LOI wickets at 23.08.

HENRY OLONGA

born Lusaka, Zambia
3 July 1976

Olonga occupies a special place in social and cricket history as the first black man to play Test cricket for Zimbabwe, just 28 months after the African republic entered Test competition in 1992. At the age of 18 he dismissed Saeed Anwar with his third delivery before becoming the first bowler since Ian Meckiff 31 years earlier to be called for throwing. With the counsel and coaching of Dennis Lillee, Olonga rebuilt his action and played 30 Test and 50 limited-over internationals between 1995 and 2003. Together with redoubtable Andy Flower he earned headlines throughout the world by mounting a black armband protest during the 2003 World Cup hosted by South Africa and Zimbabwe. The protest was made to mourn the death of democracy in Zimbabwe and a plea to stop the abuse of human rights in the country. He was compelled to leave the country and lives in exile in England.

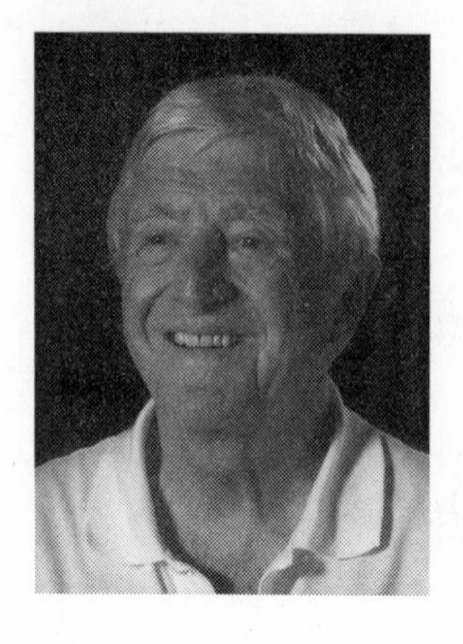

SIR MICHAEL PARKINSON

born Cudworth, Yorkshire, England
28 March 1935

Renowned journalist, broadcaster, interviewer and author, Parkinson was imbued with the spirit and love of the game from the cradle and while playing at Barnsley Cricket Club in the Yorkshire League he earned trials with the county side. His opening partner at Barnsley was Dickie Bird, who was destined to become one of the game's finest umpires, and Geoff Boycott was a teammate. 'Dickie and I thought we might play for Yorkshire, Boycott knew he would play for Yorkshire and England,' says Parkinson, who was offered but did not accept terms at Hampshire. Proud owner of two baggy green caps worn by his friend the Australian opening batsman and journalist Jack Fingleton, Parkinson relished the chance to interview cricketers on his popular chat shows. His failure to secure an interview with Sir Donald Bradman frustrated him greatly.

MANSUR ALI KHAN PATAUDI (NAWAB OF)

born Bhopal, Madhya Pradesh, India
5 January 1941

Known to his myriad admirers as 'Tiger', Pataudi generally is regarded as India's most accomplished and influential captain. Appointed to the helm at 21 and only five months after his right eye was seriously injured in a car accident in England, Pataudi engendered in his men a sense of pride and self-belief. A brilliant tactician and strategist, he boldly constructed his attack around four exceptional spin bowlers—a new and thrilling dynamic in world cricket. The son of Iftikhar Ali Khan, Nawab of Pataudi, who played for both England (in the Bodyline series) and India, he led in 40 of his 46 Test matches as India found its way in the cricket world. He scored 2793 runs at 34.91 with six centuries and learned to live with the fact that as a consequence of the accident he could never be the batsman he would have liked to have been. He died of a lung disease on 22 September 2011 aged 70.

GRAEME POLLOCK

born Durban, Natal, South Africa
27 February 1944

Arguably the game's greatest left-handed batsman, Pollock possesses the second-highest average to Don Bradman in Test cricket—60.97 (2256 runs). Restricted to 23 Tests because of the isolation of the Old South Africa, the first of his seven hundreds came at the age of 19 against Australia in Sydney in January 1964. He scored prolifically against the last two Australian teams to visit South Africa before its excommunication from the cricket community—537 runs at 76.71 in 1966–67 and 517 runs at 73.85 three years later. While absent from the traditional stage, he continued to shine in first-class cricket in South Africa and retired with 20,940 runs at 54.67 with 64 centuries. At age 43 he captivated a crowd at Port Elizabeth with a brilliant century against a rebel Australian team. His brother Peter and nephew Shaun are two of South Africa's greatest fast bowlers.

BARRY RICHARDS

born Durban, Natal, South Africa
21 July 1945

In spite of playing only four Test matches as a consequence of South Africa's isolation during the apartheid years, Richards enjoys a substantial reputation as one of the game's greatest batsmen. A glorious stroke player airily dismissive of most bowling, he flourished wherever he played: Natal, Hampshire in county cricket, South Australia for Sheffield Shield competition and in World Series Cricket. He formed a formidable opening partnership with West Indian Gordon Greenidge at Hampshire and flourished under Ian Chappell's imaginative and aggressive captaincy of South Australia in 1970–71. His brilliant and consistent scoring—1538 runs at 109.85—provided South Australia with the impetus to win the competition. He scored six centuries in 10 matches, including a monumental 356 in 372 minutes against Western Australia—325 of them in a day.

SIR VIVIAN RICHARDS

born St John's, Antigua
7 March 1952

An unabashedly proud and political cricketer, Richards was arguably the most devastating batsman of his generation. Renowned for a signature swagger and steadfastly refusing to wear a helmet against even the most fearsome bowlers, he was an intimidating force who could humiliate an attack. A charismatic soul driven by pride in his people and a passion for the game, he could change the course of a match, indeed a series, in a trice. Inflamed by England captain Tony Greig's intemperate observation that he intended to make the West Indies grovel in 1976, Richards ran amok in four Tests and scored 829 runs at 118.42, including a breathtaking 291 in the final Test at The Oval. He amassed 8540 runs at 5023 in his 121 Test appearances and succeeded Clive Lloyd as the 19th captain of the West Indies, winning 27 and losing just eight of 50 matches.

KUMAR SANGAKKARA

born Matale, Sri Lanka
27 October 1977

One of the contemporary game's most decorated players, Sangakkara was the *Wisden Almanack*'s Leading Cricketer in the World in 2011 and the International Cricket Council's (ICC) Cricketer of the Year for 2012. And to reaffirm his universal popularity, he was the ICC's People's Choice as the game's pre-eminent player in both years. A left-handed batsman of style and flair, he quickly established a reputation for a capacity to occupy the crease for long periods and score heavily. A former captain, he was at the peak of his powers in 2012 and could point to eight double centuries, leaving him behind only Brian Lara (9) and Don Bradman (12). An eloquent spokesman for Sri Lankan cricket, in 2011 he was lauded for his Cowdrey Spirit of Cricket lecture delivered at Lord's. He also regularly kept wicket and in 2012 became just the eleventh batsman to score 10,000 Test runs.

BOB SIMPSON

born Marrickville, New South Wales, Australia
3 February 1936

A fine opening batsman and among the greatest of all slips fieldsmen, Simpson boasts a unique record of service to Australian cricket over five decades. Successor to Richie Benaud as Australian captain in 1963–64, he played 52 Test matches before retiring in 1967–68. Ten years later when the game was torn asunder by the World Series Cricket revolution, Simpson returned to the fold at the age of 41 to captain and mentor a new generation. He enjoyed personal and team success against India but the might of the West Indies took its toll and he retired with 4869 runs at 46.81 with 10 hundreds from 62 Tests. In 1986 he again answered the call of despairing administrators when Australian cricket plumbed new depths. A tough taskmaster, as coach he brought a new level of discipline and determination to the Australian team and laid the foundation for a very prosperous period in both Test match and limited-overs cricket.

GRAEME SMITH

born Johannesburg, South Africa
1 February 1981

As the longest-serving captain in the annals of Test cricket, Smith has demonstrated he is as hard of head as he is hard of body. An imposing figure, he was appointed to the leadership at the age of 22 and with enormous character and courage met the challenge to rebuild the image of cricket in South Africa. He was appointed to the task in his ninth Test match, just 13 months after making his debut against Australia in March 2002. He silenced the sceptics, scoring a double century in each of his third and fourth Tests at the helm and so engineered an impressive 2–2 draw with England in his first full series. A powerful if inelegant left-handed batsman, he takes great pride in leading by example. Among his many accomplishments was to lead the Proteas to their first series victory in Australia in 2008–09. Only the indefatigable Jacques Kallis has scored more runs for South Africa.

ANDREW STRAUSS

born Johannesburg, South Africa
2 March 1977

Upright, calm and modest, Strauss's intelligent and inspirational captaincy enabled England to rise to the number one position in the Test rankings with successive Ashes series victories and a trouncing of India. A compact and highly accomplished left-handed opening batsman, he won 24 of his 50 matches in charge. Strauss made an emphatic start to his Test career with 10 hundreds in his first 30 matches and retired with 21 centuries, just one behind Geoff Boycott, Colin Cowdrey and Wally Hammond. A resolute competitor and a conspicuous respecter of the game's traditional values and virtues, he scored 7037 runs at 40.91 in exactly 100 Test matches.

SIMON TAUFEL

born St Leonards, New South Wales, Australia
21 January 1971

Appointed to umpire his first Test match at the age of 29, Taufel quickly established an impressive reputation and for five years from 2004 was named the ICC Umpire of the Year. Renowned for his communication skills and the consistency and accuracy of his decision-making, Taufel turned to umpiring after a promising career as a fast bowler was ended by a back injury. As a teenager he played in a representative schoolboys team alongside Adam Gilchrist and Michael Slater. Taufel, who survived the terror attack on the Sri Lankan team at Lahore in 2009, was 27 when appointed to his first one-day international (ODI). He retired in 2012 after standing in 74 Test matches, 174 ODIs and 34 Twenty20 matches and was appointed ICC Umpire Performance and Training Manager.

MARK TAYLOR

born Leeton, New South Wales, Australia
27 October 1964

A leader nonpareil, Taylor was one of the most accomplished batsmen of his generation. A gritty competitor, he complemented his ability as an opening batsman with freakish skills as a catcher at slip. He inherited a fine team from Allan Border and soon refined it in his name and inspired long-awaited series success in the West Indies in 1994–95 and Pakistan in 1998. In all, he won 26 of his 50 Tests in charge. The scorer of 7525 runs at 43.49, he arrested the attention of the international cricket community when he made 334 not out against Pakistan at Peshawar to equal Don Bradman's fabled hand at Leeds in 1930. Universally known as 'Tubby' because of his stocky build, he was one of the game's finest strategists and most astute diplomats—skills he deftly transferred to the commentary box when he retired after 104 Tests.

SACHIN TENDULKAR

born Bombay (now Mumbai), Maharashtra, India
24 April 1973

The peerless batsman of his time, Tendulkar is the greatest accumulator of runs in history. In all probability his achievement of 100 international hundreds constitutes a mark, like Sir Donald Bradman's Test average of 99.94, which will not be surpassed. Tendulkar made his Test debut at 16 and remained a member of the Test team at the time of his 40th birthday in April 2013. Similar in stature to Bradman, testament to his greatness was an imposing record against Australia, the pre-eminent team of his era: 3630 runs at an average of 55.00 with 11 centuries. As he officially entered mid-life he reflected on a record of 198 Test matches for 15,837 runs at 53.86 with 51 centuries and 67 fifties. A year earlier he retired from the limited-over arena after a staggering 463 appearances for 18,426 runs at 44.83 with 49 centuries and 96 fifties. At the age of 36 and 306 days he scored the first double century in one-day cricket. Intensely competitive, he is the most worshipped cricketer since Bradman.

FRANK TYSON

born Farnworth, Lancashire, England
6 February 1930

One of the fastest bowlers the game has seen, Tyson was given the sobriquet 'Typhoon' after bowling for Northamptonshire against the 1953 Australian tourists 13 months before he made his Test debut against Pakistan. The veracity of his nickname was confirmed in Australia in the summer of 1954–55 when he bowled at a terrifying pace and captured 28 wickets at 20.82 as England retained the Ashes. Injury restricted his career to 17 Tests in which he took 76 wickets at 18.56. The most affable and engaging of men, Tyson emigrated to Australia where he became a distinguished educationist. He also wrote with distinction on the game and was an insightful radio and television commentator. Into his seventies he remained closely involved in the coaching of the game in Australia and India.

DANIEL VETTORI

born Auckland, New Zealand
27 January 1979

Vettori has borne much of the responsibility for the welfare of New Zealand cricket since he became his country's youngest Test cricketer at the age of 18 years and 10 days in 1997. A guileful and indefatigable orthodox left-arm spinner, he is a member of the exclusive fraternity to have taken 300 Test wickets and scored 3000 runs. As he matured as a cricketer he had legitimate claims as an all-rounder and by the time he edged ahead of Stephen Fleming's record 111 Test appearances for the country, he could point to six Test centuries and an average of 30 batting at number eight. Given the breadth of his responsibilities, he agreed to captain for a finite period between 2007 and 2011 but like so many of his predecessors lacked support and only occasionally enjoyed success in Test matches. By dint of his versatility he has prospered at the three forms of the game and was eagerly sought by Twenty20 franchises.

DOUG WALTERS

born Dungog, New South Wales, Australia
21 December 1945

A country scallywag, Walters is a legend of Australian cricket but only partly for his deeds in the middle. Stories true and apocryphal proliferate about this gifted attacking batsman and brilliant fieldsman who invariably was portrayed as the archetypal Aussie bloke. He smoked heavily, drank consistently, played cards shrewdly and was known to take a sickie to avoid training. Having made his first-class debut for New South Wales at 17 he exploded into Test cricket scoring a century on debut against England eight days before his 20th birthday. To confirm his great promise Walters followed 155 with 22 and 115 in his second Test. Seemingly unaffected by a hiatus for two years' national service, in 1968–69 he became the first batsman to score a double century and a century in a Test match—against the West Indies at his beloved Sydney Cricket Ground, which for a time possessed a stand bearing his name. An inveterate prankster in the dressing-room he amassed 5357 runs at 48.26 with 15 centuries in 74 Tests. An eye-player conspicuously susceptible to the seaming ball in England, he also had the happy knack of taking vital wickets with his seemingly unthreatening medium-paced deliveries.

SHANE WARNE

born Ferntree Gully, Victoria, Australia
13 September 1969

Incomparable and incorrigible, Warne has strong claim to be the greatest leg-spinner of all time and in 2000 he was adjudged by an imposing panel of experts to be one of the five greatest cricketers of the 20th century. A contradictory and often controversial character, he mesmerised batsmen and captivated crowds the world over from the time he bowled the 'ball of the century' to England's Mike Gatting in 1993. With an uncanny ability to compartmentalise his life, which he thought a soap opera, Warne could intimidate with his combativeness and raw competitiveness. A cerebral cricketer with an armoury of deliveries real and imagined, he would have made a fine Test captain but for frequent lapses of judgement on and off the field. Unerringly accurate, he was the first bowler to take 700 Test wickets—96 of them (at 22.02) coming in 15 Tests in 2005. Also a highly skilled slipper, he took 708 wickets at 25.41 in a 15-year career. On 10 occasions he took 10 or more wickets in a match and whenever he bowled spectators sat forward in their seats in excitement and anticipation.

STEVE WAUGH

born Canterbury, New South Wales, Australia
2 June 1965

Statistically Australia's finest captain with 41 victories (nine losses) from 57 matches, Waugh was an uncompromising and combative cricketer who introduced the term 'mental disintegration' to the game's ancient lexicon. Introduced to the Test arena at 20 when Australian cricket was at its nadir in 1985, in his mid-thirties he led one of the country's greatest teams to a record 16 consecutive Test victories. Such was his self-discipline and determination he played a then record 168 Test matches and amassed 10,927 runs at an imposing average of 51.06 with 32 centuries. And with Dean Jones he was a most influential and innovative limited-overs player. Renowned for his philanthropy in Australia and India, during his playing days he placed great store in the game's history and initiated ceremonies and customs that have become a part of the lore of the game and have been faithfully followed by his successors.

JOHN WRIGHT

born Darfield, Canterbury, New Zealand
5 July 1954

A calm, no-nonsense, left-handed opening batsman with a deep knowledge and affection for the game, Wright was the first New Zealander to score 4000 Test runs and is, along with Stephen Fleming and Martin Crowe, the only Kiwi to reach the 5000 mark. With a game built on a sound defensive technique he was a key member of the outstanding New Zealand team which achieved significant successes against England and Australia in the mid 1980s. Entrusted with the captaincy on 14 occasions between 1987–88 and 1990 he scored 5334 runs at 37.82 with 12 hundreds in 82 Tests over 15 years. An affable soul and fine communicator, at the end of his playing career he turned his attention to coaching first with Kent in England, then with India and, more problematically, with New Zealand. His worldliness, sagacity and political savvy were evident as India coach, in which role he enjoyed considerable success, including a series win in Pakistan and memorable victories in England and Australia.

1989: incorrigible Australian batsman Dean Jones (left) elicits a gale of laughter from Prime Minister Bob Hawke during Australia's conquering tour of England. Captain Allan Border is on hand to ensure team protocols are observed.

1999: Prime Minister John Howard shares the delight of Captain Steve Waugh and his team after Australia's triumph at the World Cup in England.

CHAPTER THREE

Leadership

There has been a cordial relationship between the Australian cricket captain and his prime minister since Federation.

That the captaincy of the Test cricket team is popularly represented as the second most important office in the land can in part be attributed to the fact 10 Australian captains had been appointed before Sir Edmund Barton became the country's first prime minister in 1901.

In essence, each Australian cricket captain during the 24 years preceding nationhood symbolised an admirable figure of national importance in the eyes of those craving and agitating for Federation.

As a consequence, the 34 captains who have subsequently served occupy a privileged position in Australian society and invariably are feted by the citizenry. Everyone has an opinion of the Australian captain just as they do of the prime minister.

A healthy percentage of the country's 27 prime ministers have had a deep appreciation of the game and enjoyed a close association with the Test captain. The fact that the *Oxford Companion to Australian Cricket* includes three prime ministers and an opposition leader in its biographical list of cricket luminaries eloquently bespeaks the power and influence of cricket in Australian culture. And the *Companion* was published in 1996 before John Howard, famously branded a 'cricket tragic' by the country's 39th cricket captain, Mark Taylor, ascended to the prime ministership.

Barton, Sir Robert Menzies, Bob Hawke and former Labor leader Doc Evatt had an affinity for the game and its people and were known to use their position and influence to assist the game's governors.

As a minister in the governments of John Curtin and Ben Chifley, Evatt, a dedicated servant of the game in New South Wales, played a pivotal role in the resumption of Anglo-Australian cricket after World War II. Menzies, who offered Sir Donald Bradman the position of high commissioner to London, used his contacts and persuasiveness to ensure the Australian team visited the West Indies for the first time in 1955.

Hawke resurrected the prime minister's fixture pioneered by Menzies in 1951 for teams visiting Australia and, in an earlier incarnation as president of the Australian Council of Trades Union, informally advised Ian Chappell's Australian team on wages and work conditions.

While he was in office, Howard, who delivered the inaugural Sir Donald Bradman oration in 2000, enacted changes to the corporations law to prevent Bradman's name being exploited by the calculating and the mischievous.

Barton, a capable batsman at Sydney University in sprightly days, was well known in advance of his political career as a first-class umpire and was lauded when he defused a riot which erupted during a match between Lord Harris's England team and New South Wales in 1879. He was also a colonial selector and a vice-president of the New South Wales Cricket Association.

While it may boast a surprisingly high number of political leaders fascinated by the game, by no means is Australia the only country to have elected a 'cricket' tragic to the top job. Former British prime minister Sir John Major and Jamaican premier Michael Manley both wrote on the game with erudition. And Pervez Musharraf, Pakistan's tenth prime minister, happily engaged Howard on cricket issues at social events surrounding Commonwealth Heads of Government meetings.

'I encouraged the belief that the Australian cricket captain is the holder of the most important job outside that of the prime minister,' said Howard. 'There's a special place in Australian hearts for the Australian cricket captain. It is our national game and the person who holds that position has a status, separate and apart and, I believe, above that of any other sporting leader. That's not in any way to denigrate great sporting leaders in other sports. I don't want to denigrate any of them, they're fantastic people but because cricket is the national game it has a special place.'

Ever the realist, Steve Waugh, who has the highest winning percentage of an Australian captain to have led on more than

10 occasions—41 victories and nine losses from 57 matches—expresses another view.

'I certainly don't believe it's the second most important office in Australia,' said Waugh. 'I mean that is ridiculous. It's nice when people say that but the reality is it's far from that. It's important and it means a lot to people but, you know, you don't ever want to get too carried away with being captain of Australia and thinking you are the second most important person in Australia.'

No team sport asks more of its leader on and off the field than cricket in its purest form. Other games may make greater physical demands of its exponents but five consecutive days of intense competition creates unparalleled and often unbearable levels of mental and emotional stress.

And judging by a declaration by Sir Donald Bradman in his renowned instructional work, *The Art of Cricket,* which was first published in 1958, it has been forever thus.

'I don't know any game which entails such a severe and prolonged strain on the skipper, but, like the master of a ship, he must exercise control and accept the responsibility,' wrote Sir Donald.

Furthermore, he quoted a well-known observation of the renowned English cricket administrator and tour manager, Sir Frederick Toone, who was knighted for promoting good relations between 'the Commonwealth and Mother Country'.

Sir Frederick famously remarked: 'Cricket is a science, the study of a lifetime, in which you may exhaust yourself but never your subject.'

In one unsettling five-year period in the 1980s three Australian captains were brought to the point of emotional collapse. Greg Chappell concedes he was not in a fit state to lead when he ordered his younger brother Trevor to bowl underarm to deny New Zealand an improbable victory in a limited-overs match in Melbourne in 1981. Kim Hughes tearfully resigned the captaincy in 1984 after being brought to his knees by the ruthless West Indian fast bowlers and inept match scheduling. And two years later his successor, Allan Border, was close to a nervous breakdown in New Zealand and threatened to resign if his ragtag band did not unconditionally support him.

The game evolved so quickly and aggressively over the last 25 years of the 20th century and into the new millennium that demands on those entrusted with the captaincy increased exponentially. While the captaincy was still the ultimate prize, the office had lost some lustre and leadership crises the world over became increasingly common.

Furthermore the once inviolable office of national captain was dishonoured by notorious cheats Salim Malik (Pakistan), Mohammad Azharuddin (India), Hansie Cronje (South Africa) and Salman Butt (Pakistan) as the game confronted betting and match- and spot-fixing scandals. And suspicions were raised about others who had been entrusted with leadership responsibilities.

Moreover, in the eyes of some, the office was diminished, even devalued, by the inexorable push to appoint specialist captains for at least two forms of the game. Undeniably there was widespread angst throughout Australia when Mark Taylor, one of the greatest of all Australian leaders, was retained as

Test captain but passed over for Steve Waugh for the triangular limited-over series with South Africa and New Zealand in 1997–98. In the eyes of many the office had lost some of its preciousness.

The overwhelming success of the frenetic Twenty20 format since 2007 simply compounded the issue and raised the distinct possibility of a country presenting three national captains at any one time.

Bill Lawry, Australia's 32nd captain, is philosophical about the trend and fervently believes the status of the Test match captain is assured.

'I think you can forget 50-over and Twenty20, I don't think that rates as captaincy, really,' he said. 'I mean, you get it but you get it because you're a handy one-day cricketer and they probably think you'll do a good job. I don't think we'll remember in 20 years time who was captain of the Twenty20 World Cup. I don't think that will ever rate a mention. Not that I'm degrading the position. But it's like running a lead-up race for the Caulfield or Melbourne Cups. You know it is a stepping stone.'

Certainly only the game's most dedicated scholars will recall Lawry was Australia's first limited-over international captain in 1971 and correctly name David Hookes, Ray Bright and Ian Healy among his successors in the 50-over format.

A captain's capacity and capability at the elite level is defined by much more than tactical and strategic skill. The need to distinguish between captaincy and leadership is fundamental as is cultural and political awareness, be they the politics of cricket or party. As often as not the leader is expected to mentor or act as amateur psychologist, even surrogate parent, and behave as the public face and mouthpiece of the game if not of the country he leads. And the degree of difficulty is increased markedly where complex components of ethnicity, religion and language exist as is the case throughout the Indian subcontinent and the Caribbean archipelago.

Certainly Sir Frank Worrell and Clive Lloyd were widely considered proxy parents to the brilliant and impressionable young players from the disparate and isolated sovereign nations of the Caribbean, while Mansur Ali Khan and Sunil Gavaskar spoke often of the unique challenges of leading India with its innumerable languages, dialects and customs.

Forty-seven years after the publication of the *Art of Cricket* the gifted England captain, Michael Brearley, first published *The Art of Captaincy.* If Bradman's work is considered the definitive text on every aspect of the game, Brearley's unquestionably is the most authoritative volume on leadership.

Even the most casual of the game's observers will tell of the disparity between Bradman and Brearley as batsmen, but as captains, at least statistically, the difference is marginal. Bradman enjoyed a winning percentage of 62.50 with 15 victories and three defeats from 24 outings at the helm while Brearley points to a winning percentage of 58.06 with 18 victories and four losses from 31 matches in charge.

The power of Brearley's work is that it can be, and frequently is, applied to other spheres of endeavour well beyond the boundary—a point made in the foreword of the 2001 edition by the distinguished film director Sam Mendes, who has an abiding passion for the game.

'Personally, I find it difficult not to relate the contents of this book to what I have ended up doing for a living in the years since its publication. Maybe that's why I found myself reaching for this book looking for insights when I was in Los Angeles making *American Beauty* in 1999 and dealing with my first film crew,' wrote Mendes, who in 2012 directed the James Bond thriller, *Skyfall*.

'This book goes beyond the boundaries of the author's field and involves itself in larger discussions. What is the nature of charisma? What are its limitations? What is the place of aggression in sport? Who were the greatest captains and why? He has a talent available to very few: the ability to look again at a game that is centuries old and make us feel as if it had just been invented.'

An eminent psychoanalyst in London with a keen appreciation of the importance of introspection, Brearley has often pondered whether his love for the game and its arcane tactics heightened his interest in the way 'people ticked and didn't tick and how things happened in the mind in sport and in other areas of life.'

Certainly his admired intuitiveness as a captain begs the question whether leaders are born or can be created.

MIKE BREARLEY: Intuitive probably means going with one's hunches, one's spontaneity; not having planned everything out, worked everything out in a sort of academic way. I hope

I was intuitive in that sense. But I suppose there is also the question of how much it comes from one's nature and what one can learn. I think that is fifty-fifty. You certainly need to have certain natural qualities to be a good captain but you also need to learn tactically and how to get the best out of people. When did I understand I had the capacity to lead? I think I was always a bit bossy so I always quite liked telling people what to do. My father, a Yorkshireman, captained the club team he played for in London for a few years and always had opinions about captaincy. So I was thinking about the game from a tactical point of view from the age of seven, eight, nine, 10, you know. So I wasn't thinking about batting, bowling or fielding, I was thinking about captaincy. At school I was the best player so I was fairly naturally made the captain of teams at various points.

And I just loved the captain's tactical part of it and I think I did like the feeling of a team coming together and the feeling of helping somebody if I could, getting the best out of them. Sometimes you could and sometimes you couldn't.

Rodney Hogg, the Australian fast bowler who enjoyed stunning success against England in 1978–79 (41 wickets at 12.85 in six Tests) noted Brearley's lack of intellectual snobbery and concluded he possessed a 'degree in people'.

MIKE BREARLEY: I was flattered by that remark especially coming from someone like Rodney who didn't know me that well, personally, and we came from very different backgrounds and origins. I don't think it's always been the case. I think when I got anxious or a bit uptight or a bit critical of somebody I could get a bit snobbish or cruel or cold, which could have an intellectual component to it which I'm not very pleased about. But on the whole I don't think I came across as snobbish to all the players and they came from all sorts of backgrounds. One of them did say: 'He was alright until he started using long words and we couldn't follow it.' I think it was a joke mainly.

When I started captaining Middlesex I found it much harder to captain people who were older and had better careers than mine. I readily made contact with the younger players but I found it a bit more difficult with the older players. One of the difficulties I had was if people were critical or contemptuous of me I would react either coldly or hotly and not get the best out of them. You have to balance consultation and learning from people—finding out their ideas and knowing their feelings. You need the ability to say things straight from time to time. So the balance is the very key and depends on knowing people well. You have to be able to say things to people they don't want to hear. You have to be able to take on decisions that aren't in their personal interests; people are dropped or they don't get the new ball or they're demoted from a role in the team as they see it. Or you have to challenge them with the way they're behaving or the way they're not practising or not doing this or that or causing difficulties in the group. So you have to have the capacity and the relationship from which you can stand back. But on the other hand it's no good if you're aloof or distant. People in a team will forgive you more if you're passionately involved. You may get too angry at times or too impatient or show your feelings in a way that's not particularly helpful.

But if you can sort of say 'sorry' and get on with it and you're basically on the side of the players and the team and you show passion, I think they'll forgive you much more than if you're cold. With someone like Ian Botham I could say all sorts of things to him and he could say quite a lot to me as well but it was a productive, flowing sort of relationship. He contributed a lot, not only with his bowling and his batting and fielding but tactically as well, with ideas.

Arguably Brearley's greatest accomplishment was his masterful counselling and cajoling of Botham in 1981 when his careers as cricket captain and psychotherapist intersected. In essence, he was the architect of the only Ashes series which at every reference is preceded by a name—Botham's Ashes. Intuitively Brearley reached out to the warrior all-rounder who had been humiliated in front of a sad and silent mob at Lord's in the last of his 12 Tests as captain. Botham was eternally grateful.

IAN BOTHAM: He came up to me at the nets, at one of my rare appearances at the nets, and said: 'Beefy, can I have a little chat?'

I said: 'Of course you can.'

He said: 'Look, you've just resigned and you've got a lot of things going on. You're sure you want to play?'

And I said: 'I'm absolutely certain I want to play. I'm in great nick but I just haven't been converting it for England.

I'm in great nick, scoring lots of runs, taking lots of wickets for Somerset. Of course I want to play.'

And he said: 'Good, because I think you'll get five wickets and a hundred.' Well, he wasn't far off. [He was not. In the following Test at Headingley, Leeds, Botham returned bowling figures of 6–95 and 1–14 and innings of 50 and 149 not out and England claimed a famous victory by 18 runs.]

IAN BOTHAM: It was great, to be honest with you, because of the way it was going with the captaincy it was actually a load off my shoulders—a big, big, massive weight. I remember going back to Taunton after I'd resigned and we had a semi-final the next day [of the 55-over Benson and Hedges Cup competition] and I went for a stretch with Viv [Richards] and as I walked out on to the pitch I got a standing ovation. I thought, 'Well, okay, cool, what I've done is right.' I felt better for it and we won that semi-final and we won the Cup. It was just a great time to be around. So, yeah, happy days!

David Gower, who himself was to have a tumultuous time as England's 64th captain, was saddened but not surprised at the fall from grace of his close friend Botham.

DAVID GOWER: There was quite often a sort of prescribed succession when it came to captains and when Mike Brearley finished as captain Ian was the leading player—well established, precocious, bombastic, unplayable, irreplaceable. There are all sorts of adjectives for Ian Botham, some of them unrepeatable.

But Ian was the major figure in that team and it was largely accepted that they would give him the captaincy and see what he made of it. The fact that it all finished in not quite shame, but on a low moment for him, was a big shame, big disappointment. For him it was a catalyst to some of his most extraordinary feats on a cricket field. His reaction of course was to come out in 1981; to single-handedly turn around an entire Ashes series under Mike Brearley, who was called back to bring the steadying hand back to the tiller.

Ian wasn't really suited to captaincy for one simple reason. His innate abilities, his self-belief were of a different nature and therefore he wasn't really going to understand anyone with a weakness or with a moment of self-doubt or a problem that needed sorting or solving. He was not made for captaincy ultimately because captaincy is not just about instinct for the game. He's always had such a good instinct for the game. Yes, he can play his part instinctively as a batsman, instinctively as a bowler, instinctively as a fielder and instinctively as a suggester of ideas. But I think ultimately to be captain was not his bag.

At the age of 21 Gower, like Botham, came in to Test cricket under the steadfast leadership of Brearley and immediately fell under his spell.

DAVID GOWER: I think there is one thing that's always struck me and this has taken a while to work out. When you're young, whatever your captain says is right. But when you've got a [Ray] Illingworth leading your county side and a Brearley leading your national side, it's not just an impression. You know most of the time they were right because both of them were really good leaders with different methods, different words but very similar skills. The great skill both had was the ability to evaluate the opposition. As a player under them you just thought that every move they made was made for a good reason. You had this innate belief in them as men and as leaders.

As time moves on and you learn more about yourself and the game and develop your own understandings, then you're more ready to criticise, to challenge leaders. Brearley had this great ability to evaluate the opposition and also just to have that quiet word with his own team, with me, at suitable times. It could be just to say 'Yes, it's going well', a word of encouragement. Or it might be for a more serious chat about your abilities, your techniques, your attitudes—you know, more of a headmaster's study sort of meeting.

On my first tour down to Australia [1978–79] I remember there would be a day he would set aside for one-to-ones with all the players. It didn't have to be long necessarily. You know it could be a simple as 'Yep, form's good, yep, everything else is right?' Or if there were players with issues which might need sorting Brearley would be empathetic as well as strong. It's not just about being sympathetic or empathetic to people's plights in the team, you need to be able to understand them; to find a way to encourage a player to improve again or come out of whatever slump he might be in at that time.

Monarchist and maverick, Ian Botham was always at full stretch against Australia and was such a commanding presence in 1981 the series is known as 'Botham's Ashes'.

Spoils of victory: within three months in 1995, astute Australian captain Mark Taylor engineered series victories against England and the West Indies.

Media giant Kerry Packer and his lieutenant Tony Greig inspect the square at the Sydney Showground in 1977. Packer's 10-year-old son James is an interested bystander.

Rachael Heyhoe-Flint has dedicated her life to batting and battling for women's cricket.

Henry Olonga 'mourning the death of democracy in his beloved Zimbabwe' at the 2003 World Cup.

The inquisition: England captain David Gower flanked on his left by chief selector Ted Dexter and team manager Micky Stewart after England's fourth defeat in five Tests in 1989.

Charismatic Wes Hall has led a remarkable life. Following his distinguished career as a fearsome fast bowler he served in the Barbados parliament for 23 years and for a time was the Minister for Sport and Tourism. At 53 he became a Christian and subsequently was ordained in the Pentecostal Church. He was knighted in 2012.

One of the most poised and elegant of all batsmen, Greg Chappell exceeded Sir Donald Bradman's career aggregate when he became the sixth player to score 7000 Test runs in his 87th and final appearance in January 1984. Also a brilliant fieldsman, he held a then world record 122 catches.

Before Sachin Tendulkar it was Sunil Gavaskar who carried the sobriquet of 'Little Master'. He was the first player to reach 10,000 Test runs.

Two of the most audacious and thrilling batsmen in history, Adam Gilchrist and Viv Richards compare notes during a visit to the Bradman Museum in 2012.

Sir Garfield Sobers acted as a statesman and commentator for World Series Cricket and featured in promotional material with Australian captain Ian Chappell and West Indian skipper Clive Lloyd.

Within two years of working as a ticket collector and platform announcer for Indian Railways, MS Dhoni began an astonishing rise to the captaincy of India and fame and fortune.

Sachin Tendulkar, the most venerated cricketer since Don Bradman, on the shoulders of teammate Yusuf Pathan to celebrate India's World Cup triumph in 2011.

Unabashed patriot Steve Waugh was renowned for honouring the rich traditions of Australian cricket.

Eyes on the prize: Muttiah Muralitharan on his way to becoming the most successful bowler in Test cricket.

A thoughtful and articulate statesman for Sri Lankan cricket, Kumar Sangakkara was acclaimed the world's pre-eminent cricketer in the International Cricket Council's People's Choice Award in 2011 and 2012.

Traditionally cricket has provided a strong bond between the disparate sovereign nations of the West Indies. In the quest for unity the great cricketers of the region play under a special flag as demonstrated by Antiguan Richie Richardson (left) and Trinidadian Brian Lara.

Cold shoulder: Australian fast bowler Brett Lee—in his first Ashes campaign in 2001—at cross purposes with former England captain Mike Atherton—who was in his last after an outstanding 115-Test career spanning 12 years.

I thought Brearley was excellent at all that and I think a lot of people who played under him both at international level and Middlesex would absolutely agree with that. I wasn't ready for the captaincy although I'd had practice in the sense that I'd been Bob Willis's understudy for a year or two. So I'd had a degree of it and a bit of self-assessment, a bit of external assessment from the powers-that-be and I'd had some good advice. Yes, in that time I'd talked to all sorts of people.

For instance, I had a word with Robin Jackman, the senior pro at Surrey who came on the Australian tour of 1982–83. He'd been around for donkey's years and I think we were in Tasmania and having a drink one evening and talking about captaincy. He just said: 'Be yourself, whatever you do be yourself. Don't try and be Mike Brearley, don't try and be Bob Willis, don't try and be Ian Botham, just be yourself.' I think that is as good as it gets in terms of simple advice because as captain you have to be yourself.

The one overriding principle that I wanted to abide by was to give players responsibility for their own actions. I wanted them to think for themselves, bowlers to think of their own field placings that we could discuss, fielders to be pro-active and batsmen likewise, and for me to give them a sense that they were responsible. In some cases it was absolutely the right thing, sometimes you had to be more fatherly and sometimes more headmasterly.

It's never easy to know exactly which time is which and I wouldn't claim to have got that right throughout the games that I did captain. But there were successes, ones of which

> I'm proud, and there is that one lesson to learn—to go with yourself to back yourself. It is the best thing you can remember. Many years after Mike Brearley finished playing and I was getting towards the end of my career, I was thinking, 'Hang on, things aren't right. I've got a problem here.' My mind was not just quite right, there were doubts which I wasn't quite sure how to resolve. I went to find Mike and I said: 'I just need to talk to someone for an hour.' And I went around to his home in North London and sat there for an hour just talking. This was immensely valuable just because there was someone there that I could trust, someone I knew and had known for years and who I knew would understand.

Brearley's predecessor was Tony Greig, a favourite adopted son of the English establishment before his dramatic defection to Kerry Packer's breakaway World Series Cricket (WSC) movement in Australia. Constantly seen at Packer's side during the tumultuous developmental stages of the revolution, he was appointed to captain the WSC World XI.

> **TONY GREIG**: I was an aggressive cricketer and so you would have thought that I'd be an aggressive captain as well. But I don't think I was. I think I was relatively conservative in terms of my leadership and, you know, in hindsight, I'd like to have been different. While I'd been a captain since I was 10 years old, I've got to say that I was never brought up with anyone that gave me a captaincy philosophy. I quite envy guys like Ian Chappell who played under a captain in his

> state, Les Favell, who obviously had a huge impact on him because he was such an aggressive, positive captain. And I think there are probably others. Growing up I'd liked to have played under an Illy [Ray Illingworth] but I didn't have that exposure. So my brand was simply to do the best I could. And the best I could was somewhere in between. I wasn't overly aggressive or attacking, which I'd have loved to have been. At the same time there were occasions, I'm sure, where I was a little defensive when perhaps I shouldn't have been. So, you know, that was the way it was.
>
> But the thing that kept me going was the fact that I did perform. And I was lucky that as an all-rounder you have this wonderful opportunity and I made a serious contribution. I never had to worry about being dropped. Now that's something that I think is a big test. Quite a lot of cricketers who play international cricket get that little monkey on their shoulder and that's a tester.

He may have lamented not cutting his teeth at Ray Illingworth's direction but Greig was exposed to the reasoning and tactical acumen of the hard-nosed Yorkshireman in his formative years as a Test cricketer.

Illingworth, the antithesis of the well-connected and privileged home county chap generally expected to ascend to the captaincy at the time, garnered countless admirers when he made light of a schism within his ranks to regain the Ashes in 1970–71. It was England's first Ashes success since 1956 and the first in Australia since 1954–55. And, for good measure he retained the trophy in an absorbing series against an Australian team led by one of his admirers, Ian Chappell, in 1972. He also enjoyed series successes against the West Indies, New Zealand (on three occasions) and Pakistan.

RAY ILLINGWORTH: I always tried to get the players on-side. I always insisted we played under one rule. I used to have a meeting and say: Look, if you want to say anything now's the time to say it. You've an open market, have a go. But I don't want to hear anything outside this room that you haven't mentioned in it. So I always brought all the players into it and made them feel part and parcel of it. I think that's very important. It's also important that the players think that you know what you're doing. If they don't feel that you know what you are doing you've got problems. I always felt the players felt I knew what I was doing and I think that was very, very important.

These days I do look at team photos and there is all this backroom staff. I didn't need psychiatrists and trick cyclists and all these people. Mine was all in my head. If I'd seen a batsman play once I knew where to put a field to him. That was very, very important. I hope some of the seam bowlers, in particular, were wiser players from playing under my captaincy. Knowing the game completely and knowing the players I think is very important. I knew every player I played against. I learned from playing under a lot of different captains. Going back to my early days Norman Yardley [captain of England against Don Bradman's Invincibles in 1948] was a lovely man and a technically good captain. But he wasn't

> strong enough on players and they did what they wanted to do. That didn't work either. I played under two or three captains that I always felt pushed people one way or the other. You can't have favourites. You've got to be honest and equal with everybody. So I learned from that and so by the time I took over I think I had a pretty good knowledge of what captains were like and what they could and what they couldn't do.

True to Gower's belief that there was often prescribed succession to the leadership, the flummoxed England selectors anointed Mike Atherton as the country's 71st captain when Graham Gooch resigned after Australia completed its second victory by an innings to retain the Ashes in 1993.

Briefly in a state of reverie, Atherton recalled how at the age of 10 his father had summoned him to the television to watch Gower make his Test debut against Pakistan in 1978. Eleven years later when he played the first of his 102 Test matches, Gower was his captain. Now he was to replace Gooch, his opening partner and guide, who had succeeded Gower at the helm. The circle was complete.

> **MIKE ATHERTON**: I'd never given the captaincy much thought before accepting the job. Initial ambitions are always to try and get into the team and establish yourself and have a long career and hopefully be successful yourself and in a successful team. I don't think people going into the team think about leadership and captaincy. Certainly I didn't but lots of people said it was always going to come my way. Twenty-five

was young. I didn't think I was particularly well prepared for it in a sense. Now players are much better prepared for it, certainly for England, given the support around. But that was difficult. England had lost, I can't remember, eight, nine Test matches in a row. [It was seven losses and a draw from eight matches.] Inevitably when a captain comes in . . . Often when the team is in flux that is how you get a chance of captaincy. I didn't feel particularly well prepared. Looking back I felt a little young, a little green, a little naive. But I also knew, given I'd a bad back through my career, that I wouldn't have a long, long career. A surgeon operated on me when I was 21 and said I wouldn't be playing much into my thirties, so it wasn't a case of turning down the opportunity either. I didn't think it would come again. Keith Fletcher was the English coach at the time, a very good man and very supportive. Those were the days pre-central contracts so your support structure tended to come from your county club rather than the national team itself.

I was a Lancashire boy, born and bred. Most of the pros there were Lancashire born and bred and they were the players I'd played with in the youth system from 11 upwards. So I had very strong ties and bonds with them and really that's where the strongest support came from. I didn't cope too well with the pressures at times. I looked up to Allan Border. I'm not saying that my style was necessarily directly influenced by him but I kind of looked around at people who did the job before I took on the England captaincy and I could see an analogous situation with Border. A difficult time for Australian

> cricket for him and it was a difficult time for English cricket for me. I was looking to build something over the long term for the future and taking a lot on young shoulders to do that. It gets to you occasionally. I regret the manner in which I went about certain things but equally, I look back, 25–26 years of age . . . it's pretty young and I was pretty green, pretty naive. But looking back at those four years I think I coped pretty well. I'm not sure I could cope as well now.

England cricket has a history of its captains being born overseas—seven alone since World War II—and 34 years after Greig was elevated to the leadership another South African, Andrew Strauss, ascended to the top job. And with comparable zeal and enterprise he won 24 of his 50 matches in charge and inspired England to reach the summit of the International Cricket Council's Test match rankings.

> **ANDREW STRAUSS**: I think often in my life people saw me as a leader but I always think it's important for other people to recognise that in you rather than for you to be overly courting the leadership. My theory is that people that are courting it all the time possibly are wanting it for the wrong reasons – that it's for their own ego or their own state of mind. So I've always been, I suppose, quietly competent in that respect but when you have the full responsibility of captain of your country on your shoulders you either sink or swim. I found that it was a fillip for me and allowed me to get away from just concentrating on my batting to looking at strategy and the

structures and thinking about the players and how we could do things better. I thoroughly enjoyed it. I'm a big believer that you know how comfortable, how happy someone is off the field often translates to their performances on the field.

Being on tour for long periods challenges people emotionally and it's important they feel like they've got a support structure there for them. I remember the first talk I gave to the players was all about personal responsibility and I still fundamentally believe that to be the case. If you want guys to make smart decisions under pressure out in the middle then you've got to allow them to make decisions themselves off the field. You can't have coaches telling them what to do all the time. You need the coaches to act in a little bit more of a consultancy-type basis.

One of the big challenges of leading any group of people, I think, is you've got a lot of different individuals and you need them all to coexist in a reasonably constructive manner. I mean my feeling has always been that you set some quite rigid boundaries in place but within those boundaries you allow people to be themselves. It's important that you don't treat everyone the same. It's important that people can feel like they're doing things their way. I suppose you always think there is a right way to do things. But it's important to realise that it takes all sorts to be a successful cricket team or to be a successful organisation.

You know you need those guys that are up there and at 'em, you need those guys who love the attention and you need those guys who are the quiet achievers. You should celebrate that difference and you should allow people to be themselves, but if they overstep the mark it's important they know that it's not a free ticket. There are boundaries in place and if they overstep them then it's important they're brought back into line.

That's been a central strand to what I believe in. I read a lot of books on leadership. I read a lot of books, generally, non-fiction books, historical books. I mean I'm always fascinated. I've read a lot of books written by Winston Churchill, the way his mind worked, his great drive and commitment and desire to get things done. He was a very different character to me but I look back at someone like Martin Johnson who captained England at the Rugby World Cup in 2003. I think England's always had some great leaders in both sport and business and you learn a little bit from people. My basic philosophy is you have to be yourself. But there's always something to learn from how other people do things.

The often acute demands of captaincy can be compounded by the overtly political nature of the game in some countries. Certainly there has been documented interference by government officials in sensitive matters of governance and selection in Zimbabwe, Sri Lanka and Pakistan. It can take courage to resist those in positions of influence who have been seduced by status and power and pay lip-service to the welfare of the game and its players. Kumar Sangakkara was never cowered by the complexities and unique challenges of captaining Sri Lanka as he made clear when he so boldly delivered the Cowdrey Spirit of Cricket lecture at Lord's in 2011.

KUMAR SANGAKKARA: I think you have to enjoy the leadership because there are a lot of things about it that you don't enjoy. The one thing that keeps you going and keeps you fresh and keeps you happy is your team performing well on the field. Then you know that whatever happens outside with the petty politics and erratic administration, we are doing our job properly. It becomes a nudge, a little push for us to get better at what we do because then we're stronger than anything else.

The most important thing is to set an example for the younger players. They must understand that contrary to what people tell you or players tell you, you don't have to depend on knowing powerful people in the Board or out of the Board to play cricket in Sri Lanka. You don't need to be best friends with the chairman of selectors, don't need to eat with journalists or sit with journalists and curry favour with them. You have to depend on one thing and that is your ability to perform every single day out on the field. And the more you perform the more respect you gain. People who don't like you will not like you and people who try to manipulate you will still try to manipulate you. But if you commit to the team and the team stays strong, no outside influence can touch you. You can't say this is the same everywhere; it's just unique to Sri Lanka.

While trying to do the right thing as far as possible it is the job of the senior players in Sri Lanka to insulate the team from influences that come from the outside and so ensure that the focus is completely on playing cricket and not getting involved in power games or petty politics. I had quite a few issues with the administration and those are the things that really led me to say that I'd had enough three or four months before I quit. It was getting to a point where I didn't want to take the risk of being bitter—and bitter with my own teammates at times—because of the frustrations I had butting heads all the time over very simple things—things that were my business, involving the performance of the team and actually influenced the way we played our cricket. I thought this was not a nice way to play cricket and once I'd done my two-and-a-half-year stint as Mahela [Jayawardene] did, I said thank you and handed it over to someone fresher [Tillekeratne Dilshan] who could probably deal with things in a different way or a better way than I did.

There's always the case of the artist educating the critic and that's always been one thing I've believed in no matter what anyone says. It's all up to you at the end and you can make people change opinions. You don't have to care about them but I think it's important to know that there's a lot you can do, and when you do things people change, attitudes and opinions change. So continue doing things that you know educate the critics.

His predecessor and close friend, Mahela Jayawardene, who along with Sanath Jayasuriya is the second-longest serving Sri Lankan captain to the shrewd and politically savvy Arjuna Ranatunga, worked diligently to distance himself from the often toxic politics of Sri Lankan cricket.

MAHELA JAYAWARDENE: I take a different approach. I don't get involved in politics. No party politics and no cricket politics for me. I stand on very neutral ground and I concentrate purely on cricket. I make each and every decision purely on the basis of the good of the team and the good of the country. It is as simple as that and I try and control those things which are within my control so no one can accuse me that I was with this party or that party. I've done that from the day I joined the team.

That was something my dad told me to do because he realised what I was getting into. It has worked really well for me all these years and that was great advice from my father. I think it has helped me quite a bit because I'm good friends with everybody in the system and they also know I'm a very straightforward person who enjoys my cricket and making decisions for that purpose. So anything beyond that I let it go. I realise there are things which I can't control so I let it go and it was a much easier decision to make purely because I was a neutral.

Pakistan cricket, too, has long been characterised by tumult and instability and the inevitable meddling of officials, be they braided brass of a military regime or high-ranking bureaucrats of an ostensibly democratically elected government. It took courageous and charismatic leaders Imran Khan and Javed Miandad to stand their ground and inspire those destined to follow them.

WASIM AKRAM: My cricket, my captaincy, my personality were influenced by three men. I saw Javed Miandad early on and I learned from him how to be street smart, how to make decisions and how to think out of the box. With Imran Khan

I realised how to believe in yourself, how to believe in yourself as a cricketer or as a person. From Mudassar Nazar I picked up a cricketing mind. My philosophy was very simple—work hard and things will come your way.

If there was a single factor on which the leaders were in wholehearted agreement it was the power and profound influence of a mentor. Daniel Vettori, who so admirably led New Zealand in 32 Test matches from 2007 to 2011, spontaneously acknowledged his debt to inspirational leader Stephen Fleming, who next to Graeme Smith and Allan Border is the longest-serving leader in the annals of Test cricket.

DANIEL VETTORI: Since I stepped away from the captaincy I've talked to other guys about it and I think if you do have the desire to be captain then you have to try it. Otherwise, the ambition will eat away at you. If you've got no desire then it's better to step away from it and not be involved. But I think those guys who want to do it, who've aspired to do it, need to do it. They need to know what it feels like to captain a team because it's not the easiest thing in the world but there is a lot of enjoyment as well.

I always thought I was a role model as captain in terms of my performance. I thought I had to step it up because if you want to lead and people to follow you then you have to lead them in the right way. And I thought the best way to lead them was through performance. I learnt that from Steve Fleming and from other captains around the world. I thought

Graeme Smith, [Mahela] Jayawardene and Ricky Ponting all stepped up and scored runs when it mattered.

Bowling captains of the past always stepped up and took wickets and I thought if I was able to do that, lead with performance, then I'd get the guys to listen to me and want to follow me and to do better. I found it was a lot easier to captain the team when I was going well than vice versa. I tried to instil in the guys time and time again that whatever you do all anyone remembers is your performance. So the guys had to step up when they walked on to the park. I didn't want to worry about anything else. Tactics come and go. Philosophies come and go. But if I can get a bowler to run in as hard as he can and hit the top of the off stump as often as possible then that instantly makes me a better captain. I didn't quite appreciate how taxing the other responsibilities of captain might be and pretty early on I set myself a timeline of only four years in between World Cup cycles. As a bowling all-rounder there's so much responsibility within your own performance and then you add everything else on that captain has to do. It is quite tough. But I wouldn't have given it up. I really enjoyed doing it and I really enjoyed leading the group of guys.

I admired Stephen Fleming, who I saw intimately for over 10 years as captain, and I thought this is the way I want to captain the side and this is the person I want to be as captain. You want to do things a little bit differently and I think the fact that I was a bowler instantly meant that I was a little bit different to Stephen. But generally everything that I saw him do was something that I wanted to replicate because I thought he'd done it so well.

Arguably the most commanding and caring mentor of the contemporary game was Clive Lloyd, who marshalled and nursed his charges for 74 Test matches for a decade from 1974 as the West Indies evolved into the most irresistible force in world cricket in the 1980s.

The sheer scale of the Caribbean cricket catchment—from Jamaica 772 km south of Florida in North America by way of Trinidad and Tobago, Guyana on the South American mainland via Barbados to Antigua 692 km north of Venezuela—has always provided unique challenges for any West Indian skipper. A sense of oneness and unanimity of purpose can be difficult to attain.

Lloyd was fortunate that he began his Test career in 1966 in the company of a gifted band of cricketers who had been nurtured by Sir Frank Worrell. The first black man to captain the West Indies outside the Caribbean, Worrell was universally admired and was as much an articulate and courageous statesman as he was a skipper. He used his humanity, eloquence and the warmth of his personality to create an imposing team in his image. Seven members of Worrell's final Test team in England in August 1963 surrounded Lloyd on his debut in Bombay in December 1966. Three months later, to the day, Worrell died of leukaemia in Kingston, Jamaica.

The pervading sadness at his death increased the pressure on his successors, and Garry Sobers, himself to be knighted in 1975, and Rohan Kanhai carried the baton as best they could until

Lloyd's appointment in India in November 1974. A decade later the most powerful team in the world came under the control of the most powerful batsman of his time—the lyrically named Isaac Vivian Alexander Richards.

> **CLIVE LLOYD**: You have to work with all the ingredients—different islands, different backgrounds, different religions and all speaking differently, thinking differently. We had Hindus, we had Muslims, we had black, we had Portuguese we had a combination of races. That's why I always had a Barbadian with a Trinidadian and a Jamaican with a Guyanese and the like. That's the way you get to understand one another. And when it was possible I had a bowler and a batter. The bowler might take five wickets and he would say we need some runs here and now. So the batter knows he must play his part so you have that cohesion and they become not Guyanese and Barbadian but roommates. Michael Holding [Jamaica] and Andy Roberts [Antigua] roomed together during their careers because they got on so well you wouldn't want to break up that partnership.
>
> Really and truly it was so many things you had to get right. You had to say to the guys we have to dress properly, have to behave in a certain manner and respect not only our teammates but the people that are backing us. You have to respect the crowds and you have to sign an autograph. We were in a privileged position. As a cricketer you get everything done for you—you travel club class and you had good salaries, your food is paid for, your laundry is paid for so you have to put something back and not only into cricket but to those less fortunate.

West Indians everywhere were proud that this small 'nation' for 20 years was the best team in the world and nobody could touch them. People were proud of us because we were not snobbish, we would sign autographs we would do anything to please people. We were happy, they were happy, the Caribbean was happy. Cricket is a very important part of our structure and we need to bring that back. We need to get people together and thinking as one. You know Guyana has got the right motto: 'One people, one nation, one destiny.' That's what the West Indies should be. If it's possible we should have one flag, one anthem and a motto for all. We are one although we are spread round and we play as one. I learnt from the mistakes we made in the past so it was important for me to pass that on. That is what we need to do with our young players. If you don't know where you come from you don't know where you're going. You must respect what other people have done.

VIV RICHARDS: I was very proud to be captain because I felt Clive Lloyd did a magnificent job in helping to gel us together. You'll have folks who will say he had a great team. I wouldn't buy that particular argument. I wouldn't buy that one bit. Great teams sometimes need controlling and when you have a great team coming out of the Caribbean you are going to have so many different personalities. I felt he did a magnificent job, just his demeanour, the way in which he helped us to gel. Clive didn't inherit a great team he helped to create a great team.

So the journey started with the leadership role and when I was given the opportunity to lead I felt that I had to carry the baton. I wanted to do it my way but certainly there was a platform in order for us to do things. Not the old sporadic way with everyone doing their own thing but in a way that had been successful. Why not carry the successful plan forward? I felt it my duty to uphold what had been started and maybe that's why I went on and captained in 50 Test matches. I was fortunate enough not to have lost a series and this is all down to individuals who are part of your team—the camaraderie, the collectiveness. I'm proud of that—you know, it's like carrying the baton. I never felt by myself.

I was proud being the West Indies captain. I had an important act to follow. Clive showed the way in which all this should be done and I had a duty to uphold the practices to keep us fully united even though we did have our differences. In any team you are going to have folks with little differences. I'm extremely proud of the blueprint which was set out for people like myself. It's a pity that later generations didn't quite fulfil these roles . . . about carrying the baton. It is a bit slippery at the moment, very slippery, it gets into hands and falls out. So being that slippery we have go to find someone who can hold that baton and run with it the way the godfather of captaincy, Clive Lloyd, did.

Lloyd's first series as captain coincided with the last by his opposite number, Mansur Ali Khan Pataudi, who despite the loss of the sight of his right eye in a car accident as a young man had risen to being one of India's finest batsmen and a leader nonpareil in 40 Test matches between 1962 and 1975. His father, the Nawab of Pataudi senior (Iftikhar Ali Khan), who played three Tests for England—including two in the infamous Bodyline series of 1932–33—also had the distinction of leading India on three occasions in 1946.

The frustrations expressed by Lloyd and his predecessors resonated with Pataudi and his successors, who perennially confronted problems and challenges unique to India.

> **MANSUR ALI KHAN PATAUDI**: Captaining India is not very easy. Captaining any team is not easy but India is particularly difficult—different backgrounds, different languages, different food habits, all those different cultures. I think the best thing to do was to remain as fair as you could to ensure that people never felt that you were being in any way biased or unfair or you were selecting on a personal basis or something of the like. And, of course, you had to be pretty strong on your strategy and tactics. I think you have to understand the game and they [the players] have to realise, and they did realise, that this chap understands.
>
> India had just achieved independence and we were lacking a certain amount in confidence, especially against the white races. I think my first job was to ensure that this lack of confidence, this kind of complex, was dissolved pretty quickly. You have to study, you have to read, and you have to look at your mistakes. You have to read about other situations, how people reacted how the captains thought.

Instinct to me is a mixture of experience and a mixture of common sense.

SUNIL GAVASKAR: Because we come from a huge country with about eight or 10 major languages and maybe a hundred dialects and different cricketing cultures, I insisted only two languages be spoken in the dressing-room—Hindi, which was the common language, or English. Nobody was going to speak any other language even to somebody from his own state or his own city. If he was going to have a chat in the Indian dressing-room it had to be in Hindi or English because I didn't want any player to feel he was being talked about by his teammates.

We had a team which was pretty good in terms of self-belief. There were players like Gundappa Viswanath, Kapil Dev—a match-winner with both bat and ball—and we had some world-class spin bowlers and some very determined young players coming through. So we had a pretty well-balanced team and a team that believed in itself. So really, as captain, it wasn't too tough to handle because we all had a common goal and that was to win for India and, you know, to bring glory to India.

KAPIL DEV: I was too young, too young. I was 22 years old. You don't know your mind, you don't know half the things. I think the Board was wrong, totally wrong at that stage. They should not have made me captain. I was too young. A boy, I wouldn't say a man. And when you have a cricketer in the team who is 10 years senior and they make you captain because you have ability . . . Our cricket Board always wants to control the cricketers so they keep changing the captains to get control of the team, which is wrong. I thought they made me [captain] a little early and they removed me a little early.

My father and mother were farmers who didn't know the name of cricket. After the Partition of India they came from the other side of what they call Pakistan so we were village farmers and living in the city and we did what the city boys do. I came from a family who I would say had to survive themselves.

MS DHONI: If I never dreamt of playing for the country then I would be lying if I said I wanted to be captain. It just came upon me, you know. They gave me the job. For me captainship is an added responsibility. It's something that the selectors and the BCCI [Board of Control for Cricket in India] think I can do. That's why I've been given the job. It's a job profile more than a position. I want to stick on to it to do something for my country. If it's not working somebody else needs to do it because ultimately what's important is for the Indian team to do well.

The country's name is at stake. I try to be honest—that's the one thing I'm very particular about. I try to be fair in whatever decision I take and no human emotions should come and affect that feeling. I try to keep things simple and do things that are in the best interests of the team and get the players

> together in the right attitude. And it's tough at times. So I'm the captain who has to realise what are the problems in a particular game and generalise the solutions. I just generalise it for the best interests of the team and I've been blessed with a very good side. All of them put in a lot of effort, you know. It's not always the result that's important. I think that way I'm very blessed. As captain I think Test cricket is slightly tougher compared to the other two formats, the reason being the time span. I always felt Test cricket is something that's a bit tough to captain especially outside India.

Given the often emotional binds of history and the richness of ritual, Australia and England traditionally have accorded Test match captains greater recognition and privileged social status. They are citizens of distinction feted long after they have left the game and often are the recipients of government decorations.

Furthermore the expansive and sophisticated television appreciation of the game since the brusque intervention of media mogul Kerry Packer in the late 1970s has provided many former captains with a medium to remain intimately involved in the game and therefore in the public gaze and consciousness.

And so comprehensive is the media coverage of the contemporary game that irrespective of time, place and context the view of any erstwhile Test captain is considered credible and valuable and is regularly sought and circulated.

> **STEVE WAUGH**: I had the luxury and freedom of developing my own game before I became captain and that's a big positive

for any captain. You know, I felt a little bit for people like Graeme Smith [South Africa] and Stephen Fleming [New Zealand] who got thrown the captaincy at a young age.

I think it's almost impossible to captain a cricket team at a young age because, one, you don't know yourself, two, you don't know your game and, three, it's hard to man-manage 15 people because the captain's role was basically that in those days. It's changed a bit now but you really have to manage a whole lot of different personalities and egos and if you are not experienced in life situations it's a tough job. I think I was really well prepared to take it on.

I never really sought the role. It wasn't something I was desperate to get. If it came along it came along. I knew my game really well and I knew I could captain the side. I had the nous to do it and I think I had the instinct to do it. I was ready so I guess in a lot of ways I was lucky. It was almost perfect timing.

I'm an observer of a lot of stuff. Although I don't study people intensely I observe. I learned what does work and how to manage players and expectations. And I learnt most of this from losing. Actually, I don't think you learn a lot from winning. I learnt the tough facts about being an international cricketer and what it takes to be a good cricketer and a good team from losing. It's almost a checklist of what not to do. And then, when you are winning, you get the feel or vibe of what you are doing well and try and remember it.

Ultimately I had to captain my way and that's something that took a little bit of time. I think I was captaining by consensus and trying to please everyone because I'd been one of the boys for 14 or 15 years. It's a big change, you know, from mucking around and pulling pranks and being on the social committees to all of a sudden being captain. The role has changed a lot so it took me a little while to get used to the change.

I like to empower people, to give them opportunities. I think I listen and I like to observe. It's all about putting people in positions they're probably not accustomed to. I would like to think that by challenging them and putting them in different situations, I made people believe they could do things they didn't even think possible themselves—treating people equally but differently. You know there's non-negotiables like being on time and wearing the right uniform but then trying to push the buttons to make them the best cricketers and, I guess, the best people they can possibly be. Some people were very low maintenance and some people were high maintenance. Other people you had to give confidence to in the media. It was about pushing the right buttons. I think a leader is about listening and observing.

I think it's somewhat overstated when people say the great leaders are the ones who make fantastic speeches and these great hand gestures on the field. I think a lot of times the good or the great leaders are really subdued and quiet. There might be one quiet word away from the game or something you say at a meeting. I was more the one-on-one stuff away from the game. I was never big on the big speeches before the game. I felt players were there because they were good players and didn't need too much talking to at that level. It might be just a couple of words here or there. So it was about backing people and always being positive and having that goal or the team vision. You had to give people with individual flair opportunities but at the end of the day we had to try and achieve something as a team.

RICHIE BENAUD: The only reason I became captain was because Ian Craig got hepatitis. He was very unlucky. He got hepatitis and he tried to play on and it didn't work so he realised then that he just had to drop out. Now at the same time Neil Harvey did a television interview in Melbourne saying he was going to move to Sydney for work. And when he arrived I'd just been made captain of New South Wales for the first match in Brisbane. It wasn't going to be a situation where Neil would move house and then be captain of New South Wales. New South Wales–Victoria things didn't stretch that far! Now you've got all sorts of little bits and pieces.

So I captained the first match in Brisbane and Neil makes a hundred. We come back down and England are coming round on the bottom bit of Australia and then there was the Australian XI match at the Sydney Cricket Ground. Freddie Trueman's footholds gave Tony Lock the chance to bowl out the Australian XI twice and Neil, captaining the side, therefore was beaten. Don't forget about those footholds. They stuck in my mind.

Now we had a situation. Harv and I were having lunch together at the Cricketers' Club the day the captaincy was announced and it came to me. I was captain according to the announcement and Harv reached across the table and shook hands and said 'Good luck, I'm with you. We just want to avenge that 1956 business' [a 2–1 Ashes defeat]. So we got on well then and he was a wonderful vice-captain. He was a brainy cricketer as well as being one of the greatest batsmen the world has ever seen. I'd go and ask him things or he would come and say things to me. We were that good mates and we remained so.

We went through winning and losing stretches, happy and unhappy times but we've always been good loyal friends and still are to this day. When you go through all the captains the successful ones have been lucky. I'm not saying luck outweighed it but once when asked about prerequisites for an outstanding Test captain I said: It's 90 per cent luck and 10 per cent skill. Just make sure you've got the 10 per cent or you might as well go home.

IAN CHAPPELL: If I was asking for their loyalty as a captain I thought it was only fair I should return it in the same vein. I think it's part of what our players want out of a captain. You've got to earn their respect. I think that's probably, if not the most important, it is one of the two most important characteristics. The other thing they want from you is honesty. If I'm asking them to bust a boiler on the field they expect me to be busting one for them.

I'm not sure when I came up with the quote but I did say that once you're their captain you're their captain for all time. I've always felt that. If there is a cricketer in trouble, particularly one that I respect, I'll try and do something to help. And they don't have to have played under me. But, you know, it's a bit more so if you've captained them. All of those guys did something to enhance my record as a captain so why am I just going to brush them [off] if they're in trouble. When I was captain of Australia there was no players' association so there was no one there to fight the fight for the players. I always thought if they give me 100 per cent out on the field then I've got to return the compliment off the field. And the Australian captain was the only one who could fight those battles.

Now that's not to say I didn't enjoy having a stoush with the administrators from time to time. When I see things that are wrong, particularly things that are going to impinge on the winning of a cricket match, I want the problem fixed. And particularly a team that I am captaining, so therefore all the Ws and Ls are going against my name. And I don't want it fixed in six months or 12 months I want it fixed now. That was my attitude to the Board and they'd say: 'Oh, yes, Ian, we'll work on that.' Don't work on it just get it fixed because it is going to make a difference to us winning or losing. So, really, rather than thinking that I was going to change the game in any radical way that was the fight I had to fight as Australian captain. Then I retired and an offer from World Series Cricket came along and I thought well, this is something that I believe [in] and I've probably got a little bit of cricket left in me and it's something worth fighting for.

That was as far as my thinking went, really. The fact it did end up dramatically changing the game and there were 50 odd players that signed with World Series Cricket and I think everybody played their part. I think I probably get too much credit for World Series Cricket and Dennis Lillee certainly doesn't get enough. Probably without Dennis Lillee World Series Cricket may never have happened.

MARK TAYLOR: Captaining or leading the team is a mile from your thoughts when you come into a side. Your first thought is to do enough to maintain your spot in the side. Then, when you get to that stage, you start to think, okay, I want to become a dominant player, the best player I can be. I think once you achieve that and you get to a stage where you think, okay, I'm now a bit of a regular, you then think to yourself, do you want to become a leader? Do I think I can become a leader? Do I know the game well enough?

Probably during the early 90s I was always thinking about who I'd bowl, where I would put a fieldsman. I think every player should think like that to be totally honest and not enough do. I don't think I ever aspired to be a leader and I was a little bit surprised when I got a phone call in 1992 before the Sri Lankan tour to take over from Geoff Marsh who was vice-captain. I don't think I ever thought it was going to happen but I wasn't shocked either because I thought I had something to offer as a leader because A: I didn't bowl B: I was an opening batsman and C: I fielded at slip, which I think is a great place to watch the game.

As vice-captain to Allan Border on the 1993 Ashes tour I got to captain a few games and do things the way I thought was right. AB left me to do my own thing and that was, in hindsight, very generous of him because that's what should happen. I think if a guy takes over he should be left to his own devices. If he needs help a captain should be prepared to ask for help but be left to captain the side the way he feels is right. The only real piece of advice I ever got from AB was to captain my way. So taking over from AB was not daunting because he had given me a side that was playing well. We weren't considered the best in the world but we were close. I was lucky to take over then but I was also very mindful not to captain as AB would do it. I wanted to have my own way of doing things and went about doing it the way I thought I wanted to captain the side. I think my philosophy of captaining certainly developed. I didn't realise the announcement of my appointment was going to have such an impact.

All of a sudden I was asked how I was going to take the team forward and what my philosophy was and I didn't really have anything planned. I remember saying that the team were not going to be pussycats under my captaincy and that was the headline the next day. So I learnt to captain the side by the old 'school of hard knocks' and you said what you thought but with certain reservations. Obviously you worked out very quickly that if you said something that was slightly controversial you could bet it would end up in the news the next day.

There is a difference between being a captain and a leader. I think every person who plays in the Australian cricket side should be a leader because you've been picked from various states or provinces into a representative cricket team. So, really, you are a leader—you're a leader of your own country from that point of view. Captaincy is different because all of a sudden you become the leader of the leaders and I think that's an interesting way to look at it when you take over the captaincy. You are not necessarily going to know everything about the game because the other 11 guys around you also know a lot about cricket. So I think it's important that you tap into them, make sure you work with them because they're going to be very helpful to you. But also be prepared to make a decision which doesn't always make them feel happy or make them all agree with you. That's what captaincy is all about—finding a way of working with those other leaders in your team for the good of the game. And that may not be in the best interests of all the players who are around you. And the more you keep the game simple the better you'll be.

ADAM GILCHRIST: Such is my personality type I don't know that I would have been able to captain for a sustained period. I might not have been able to be a Test captain. The wicketkeeping aspect has got nothing to do with it. Take that away and it's more the person and personality and how you go about things; how you handle the highs, the lows, the criticisms, the difficulties. I'm not sure that as a personality I would have been the greatest at that. I know all of that would have filtered into my personal game. That doesn't tell me a wicketkeeper/batsman couldn't do it. MS Dhoni from India has shown a remarkable ability to do it. It depends on what price you put on the various aspects of your game and how you can balance all of that up. To captain successfully for a sustained period has more to do with the personality than the player type.

I assumed the vice-captaincy a little by default with the administrators feeling that no longer should it be with Shane Warne and they didn't feel Ricky [Ponting] was right at that moment. So I was probably in the right place at the right time. I never coveted the position but it was a very proud moment, and still is, to say I captained my country. Yes, it is true that my wife, Mel, cajoled me into taking the job in India. I didn't want it. I was nervous. I had a bit of baggage from our unbelievable tour there in 2001. By the end of that tour I was an emotional wreck. Probably not that drastic but I had a lot to think about whenever I went back to that country for Test cricket.

The moment Ricky broke his thumb against England in the semi-final of the Champion's Trophy at Edgbaston I started panicking. That game wasn't even over and the tour hadn't even been finalised. Mel encouraged me and settled me down. It turned out to be one of the greatest challenges—probably the pinnacle of my cricket career. The challenge of captaining took away my worries about my own game, my self-doubt. I was more concerned about the other 13 players and support staff on the tour.

When you score your first Test century or get your first Test cap you think about all those people who helped you get there. When we won in Nagpur in 2004 I felt just exactly that: Steve Waugh, who had contributed so much to that player group, had retired by that point; Ricky [Ponting] was injured but was there on the sidelines; John Buchanan, who had held us all together and challenged us. India was like a John Buchanan—it would continually challenge you, test you. But when you succeeded as a result of those challenges it was the most fulfilling moment in my cricket career, I think. But I would never lay claim to saying it was because I was captain that we won. Far from it. But it is a nice footnote to that victory to say that I walked out and tossed the coin and led that team onto the field through that winning period. So, yes, it helped me move on from some little personal demons.

ALLAN BORDER: Initially I was reluctant. I wasn't sure that I was the right bloke, whether I wanted to do it. I was quite happy being one of the boys so that affected captaincy and leadership. I think captaincy on the field is pretty routine. Marshalling the troops out on the field is one thing. It's more what goes on behind the scenes that's probably more important. And to be honest, initially, I wasn't very good in that area.

When a philosophy starts to develop you realise you have to take this role a bit more front-on. You've got to be a bit more of a leader behind the scenes. Then I did start to think it was about creating an atmosphere—an atmosphere where people could play at their best. I tried to promote that environment where players were happy and enjoying themselves. Obviously disciplines are important because you can't let certain little things develop that are not for the team. So philosophies did, I think, develop over time. That was my situation. I got better as I evolved as a captain over a 10-year period. I don't think you've got those luxuries in the modern world. I think you've got to get into the job and, boom, develop your own style straight away. I think I was given a three- or four-year ride initially to work into becoming a better leader stroke captain.

The Captain Grumpy tag? Oh, look, I think it was justified in the difficult times in the first three or four years as captain. I'm a very hard marker of myself, my own performance and that sort of spills over into team performance. I just don't like failure, particularly if you feel you haven't given it your best. I just felt that was the situation at that period and I could have been doing better. I was probably aware that I wasn't being the captain and leader I should have been and that our performances both personally and collectively weren't up to scratch. So that came out, I suppose, when you have to front the media and some of the questioning is difficult at times. There was a certain grumpiness to my demeanour through that period so it is a justifiable tag. But I think I had a pretty good relationship with the cricketing media but sometimes the external media was more difficult. But generally I think I was pretty fairly treated.

GREG CHAPPELL: Perhaps I wasn't smart enough to realise I could have been disadvantaged following my brother as captain. In hindsight it may have been better if there had been a gap between the two of us. As Ian once said we're a lot closer than most people realise but there is a difference. Perhaps because I'm the second sibling I had a chance to view his indomitable spirit from a distance and realise that it might be a good idea to just open the door and go through it rather than run through the wall. So I softened a little bit in that regard. But, no, I don't think I was under great pressure because of Ian's reputation. I think I only had benefits from being the younger brother and Ian being the man who sort of cleared the path in front of me and made it a lot easier for me. I mean, he was a very good captain, there's no doubt about that.

We had our moments, we still have our moments. I mean we grew up as brothers, for goodness sake, and fairly combative ones at that. We've been arguing for as long as I can remember and we had our arguments on the field. But I didn't disagree with him too often. I might have challenged him a few times but there weren't too many times other than the odd occasion when I thought I should have been bowling. We didn't have too many problems on the field. I knew he was the boss and apart from the fact he was my brother he was the captain and that in itself meant that he had to be respected.

He was the one who inspired me a lot. You know our father was the one who gave me the love of the game. But seeing Ian have success in the game, certainly once he started playing international cricket, made me think maybe I could do it. So, you know, he made it easier for me in more ways than he made it difficult.

The darkest day: a graphic image of terrorists attacking buses carrying Sri Lanka's finest cricketers and Test match officials outside the Gaddafi Stadium in Lahore, Pakistan, in 2009.

Australian opening batsman Rick McCosker (left) and Indian leg-spinner Anil Kumble (right) defy the searing pain of a broken jaw to fulfil Test match obligations.

CHAPTER FOUR

Badge of courage

Life is mostly froth and bubble,
Two things stand like stone,
Kindness in another's trouble,
Courage in your own.
—Adam Lindsay Gordon

From time immemorial cricketers have required moral and physical courage to play and prosper. By its very nature and rich history, cricket is more demanding of its players than perhaps any other sport.

It is an ancient game which trumpets its traditional values and virtues and has enshrined in its laws codes of conduct and the ideal spirit to be invoked for participation.

The fragmentation and adulteration of the game since the tumultuous 1970s and 1980s, have seen professionals of the new era confronted with unprecedented moral and physical challenges, dilemmas and dangers.

The deeply conservative game was first abruptly shifted from its axis in 1977 when charismatic England captain Tony Greig affronted the establishment everywhere—and in England in particular—by aligning himself with media mogul Kerry Packer and the World Series Cricket movement.

Once thought to be impregnable, the Lord's establishment was breached again in the 1990s when years of relentless if undemonstrative lobbying by irrepressible former England women's cricket captain Rachael Heyhoe-Flint finally earned women the right to membership at the home of the game as the 21st century dawned.

Henry Olonga, the first black man to play Test cricket for Zimbabwe, risked his life and perhaps the lives of family members by protesting the regime of despotic Zimbabwean president Robert Mugabe during the 2003 World Cup, which was staged in Zimbabwe, South Africa and Kenya. Another black fast bowler, legendary West Indian Wes Hall, once stood his ground with cricket-loving Australian prime minister Sir Robert Menzies.

The 2003 World Cup is also remembered for redoubtable Adam Gilchrist showing the courage of his convictions and walking when adjudged to be not out in a semi-final with Sri Lanka at Port Elizabeth.

Six years later the game lost its last vestiges of innocence when terrorists attacked the Sri Lankan Test team and match officials as they were being driven to the Gaddafi Stadium in Lahore for the third day of the second Test with Pakistan.

Muttiah Muralitharan, once described as the most harangued cricketer since Douglas Jardine because of his radical bowling action, was one of the frightened players sprayed with glass and the blood of teammates.

It was an appalling act of violence that for former England captain and distinguished broadcaster David Gower revived memories of his fraught mission to India in 1984 when Indian prime minister Indira Gandhi and the deputy British high commissioner Percy Norris were assassinated.

Physical courage has always been required to play the game and tales of defiance and bravery have been a part of the lore of the game since Charles Bannerman retired hurt with a split finger after scoring the first Test match century in the inaugural Test match at the Melbourne Cricket Ground in 1877.

At the same arena a hundred years later another Australian opening batsman, Rick McCosker, provided an unforgettable memory batting at number 10 with his broken jaw swathed in bandages. In 2002, Anil Kumble, who was destined to lead India, bowled 14 overs with a broken jaw and captured the wicket of Brian Lara in a Test match in the West Indies. Like Sachin Tendulkar and Mansur Ali Khan before him, Kumble had found something deep within himself that enabled him to defy pain and answer his country's call.

The 'black armband' protest by Olonga and Andy Flower 'mourning the death of democracy in our beloved Zimbabwe'

caused a furore for the International Cricket Council which staged the blue-riband World Cup in Africa for the first time in 2003.

Zambian-born Olonga, whose Test career ended just weeks before the opening ceremony of the World Cup, had carried the hopes and aspirations of black Zimbabweans since making his Test debut against Pakistan at the age of 18 in 1995.

His debut, however, was mired in controversy when he was no-balled for throwing after dismissing Saeed Anwar with his third delivery and he bowled only 10 of Zimbabwe's 186 overs in their famous first Test victory.

With the help of a triumvirate of fast bowling champions—Dennis Lillee, Joel Garner and Clive Rice—Olonga rebuilt his action and took 68 wickets at 38.52 in 30 Test matches until November 2002.

The enduring black armband protest against Namibia in the opening match of the World Cup at Harare generated publicity throughout the cricket world and far beyond and resulted in Olonga being expelled by his club Takashinga. Persona non grata with the Zimbabwean authorities, he reappeared only once during the tournament and made his 50th and final limited-over international appearance against Kenya at Bloemfontein on 12 March. He then hurriedly left the country to live in exile in England and by 2013 still had not returned to Zimbabwe.

HENRY OLONGA: When I wrote my book, my autobiography called *Blood, Sweat and Treason*, I had to confront my whole life, if you will, in the space of 100,000 words. I had to relive a lot of things and the build-up towards this black armband stance because a lot of people, including myself, I suppose, for a long time just focused on the stance itself and forgot or didn't pay attention to the number of steps that it took to get me there. I don't want to regurgitate what happened but a couple of things played a role in getting me to a place where I was willing to take the stance against the regime in Zimbabwe. Of course, there were the human rights abuses that have occurred in Zimbabwe since the early eighties when Robert Mugabe first came to power. It's well documented on the internet and all over the world and you can find out what that all entailed. But basically, in a nutshell, tens of thousands of people lost their lives in what some people would call an ethnic cleansing. I don't know what you want to call it but some have called it genocide. But either way a lot of people lost their lives unnecessarily.

So there was that and there was also corruption in government. There was my faith, which had a part to play in it, of course. Something else that had a role to play was that I was asked to be the patron of an orphanage. I know there is corruption all over the world but in Africa it's through the roof and off the charts and Zimbabwe is no exception. We had corruption at the highest levels and for a number of years. One of the things that really annoyed me was the fact that we had government ministers who were buying new houses, getting new cars every few months because they're filthy rich and yet the vulnerable people in society, widows, orphans, very rarely saw any significant money coming their way through the national budget. But we were spending tens of thousands, millions even, on defence and we were fighting a war we had no business fighting in the Democratic Republic of Congo. Those things, put them all together, made me a little angry, a little upset and I felt I needed to do something.

So my opportunity came when Mr Flower and myself met for a coffee one day or lunch, I can't remember, and we mused [on] the idea of doing a kind of protest prior to the World Cup of 2003. We weren't sure how we were going to do it. Initially it was to boycott the whole thing and Andy was trying to get me to enlist some of the black players in the side because he didn't think he could.

A long story short, in the end we decided just the two of us would do it. There was no point in trying to get the rest of the team because, first of all, some people wouldn't want to do it and some of the guys were young and we didn't want to endanger their careers or their lives. Andy and I met with a few people, consulted with a few important folk like David Coulthard, who was a senator actually at this point in time in Zimbabwe, and wrote a statement. David's a lawyer so he helped us draft it so we wouldn't fall foul of the powers-that-be, or so we thought. It didn't make any difference that we worded it legally correctly. Then we did it in the first match we played in the World Cup [versus Namibia in Harare on 10 February].

We went on the field with these black armbands on and a lot of people think they were really well-groomed armbands sewn together by our parents. No, it was just a piece of insulation tape, electrical insulation tape you probably couldn't even see. And I get into all this trouble just because of a little piece of insulation tape wrapped around my arm. And, of course, my life changed, didn't it? I got death threats and was dropped from the side.

I had to leave the country and haven't been back. I'm an exile living in England because of the protest we did and, you know, I would do it again. I think it was the right thing to do. What did change? Probably nothing! But in the words of Sir Edmund Burke [18th-century Irish philosopher and statesman]:

All that's necessary for evil to prosper
is for good men to do nothing.

I'm not going to say that Mr Flower and myself are good men but, we felt we couldn't do nothing. Andy came to me. He'd been approached by someone else who convinced him that something needed to be said at the World Cup. If I'm not mistaken this gentleman appealed to the South African era of apartheid when there were sporting boycotts and the motto of the ANC [African National Congress] was 'no normal sport in an abnormal country' and he used those words and convinced Andy to approach me.

It was always a risk that when the stance was taken our lives would be in danger. It's true that we met with a few people who basically advised us on what the possible fallout would be and one of those things that we had to deal with was the possibility of getting killed. We thought it was remote but there was a chance that that might happen. But we were also advised that we might go to prison, get framed for crimes we didn't do. I mean they're tactics that governments use. This is not popular me saying this, but governments if they want to get you they can. We had to be aware of that but we felt that under the light, the spotlight of the . . . World Cup . . . they wouldn't dare do anything.

You know people will always ask should sport and politics mix. Right now I'm not a fan of sport and politics necessarily mixing. You know, I wouldn't want a politician to get involved in the running of a sport, that sort of thing and interfering. I'm not a fan of that. But Zimbabwe was not a normal country at that time and I still don't think it's a normal country. Things are getting better now, there's no doubt about that, but the regime is guilty of gross human rights violations and we wanted to make that clear to people who didn't know.

One of the most amusing things that came out of the ICC not sanctioning us was that my club, Takashinga, said that I had brought the game into disrepute. So they banned me effectively from playing for them after the black armband stance. I thought how ironic that the highest body finds us not guilty.

They asked us not to do it again, of course, and they deferred the decision to the local board so the Zimbabwe Cricket Union were then empowered. They instructed us not to do anything like that again but they didn't quite word it correctly. So we wore white armbands after that, then we wore a red one and eventually they said don't wear anything that conflicts with our official gear. So that put a lid on that.

The ICC would have copped so much flak, I think; millions of people resonated with the message that we had.

Throw aside the whole argument of sport and politics mixing just for a second. As a human being you've got people who've been murdered, tortured, raped, plundered, pillaged by a government that's all-powerful and you've got a couple of cricketers who were powerless themselves who are saying, come on guys, stop this nonsense. Prove to me that that's wrong. One of the benefits is the media embraced the stance. They talked about it and continued to ask questions of the regime in Zimbabwe. I think governments need to be kept honest. They need to be held to account. They need to be transparent and the media does that, doesn't it? It asks questions that no one else asks so it keeps them honest in areas that they would have stuff to hide. So clearly there was a focus of attention, the spotlight, if you will, on Zimbabwe even if it was just for the period of the World Cup. As a result of coming to England I was allowed to speak more and more about my stance, about my story and a lot of people were educated by the media that surrounded the black armband stance.

So, if you asked me what we achieved it would be that: That there was attention focused on the country. Did it change anything? Of course not! If you look at Zimbabwe, Mugabe's still in charge and worse things were done after the stance. Did we change some things? I believe maybe we did. Maybe we changed the hearts of people who were initially ignorant of the issues in Zimbabwe. Maybe we educated a few ignorant people. I don't know, but I hope we achieved some things that we set out to do.

The game of cricket as generations have known it changed irrevocably on 3 March 2009 when buses carrying the Sri Lankan cricket team and umpires and other match officials were ambushed by terrorists near the Liberty Roundabout on approach to the Gaddafi Stadium in the Pakistan city of Lahore.

For more than 10 minutes bullets rained on the players' 60-seater bus and the minibus carrying the terrified officials. Eight people were killed and 20 injured, including Sri Lankan players Tharanga Paranavitana and Thilan Samaraweera and umpire Ahsan Raza. An unknown number of attackers left behind a large cache of weapons including a rocket launcher, anti-personnel mines and unexploded car bombs.

KUMAR SANGAKKARA: It was strange because in Sri Lanka cricket was above everything else. We would never be targets of terrorism. But Pakistan was possibly different when the tour was arranged by the then chairman [of Sri Lanka Cricket] Arjuna Ranatunga. You know, we wrote an email, we actually drafted an email. We were in Bangladesh at the time and we had a team discussion the moment we heard that the tour was [happening]. But there was no way we could get it changed or cancelled or anything like that because the relationship between the countries went beyond cricket at that time, especially in the war environment we had.

We wanted certain points addressed and one was security. We wanted an independent [person] to give an assessment, we wanted insurance for the players going to Pakistan and we wanted to spend some time with our families before we left. And we wondered whether the tour could be shortened. Rather than playing three Test matches, three one-dayers and two Twenty20s we could play one Test match and two one-dayers because we were actually doing them a favour by going to Pakistan when no one wanted to.

So we actually sat down and Mahela [Jayawardene] and I drafted an email which we sent to the Board by eleven o'clock at night. By twelve o'clock or before 2 pm the next day we had a reply from the Board saying that the security assessment had been done, it's fine, insurance, you'll have to get it on your own, no time to spend with your families and we had to go straight from Bangladesh. And now the Pakistan Cricket Board [was] requesting to play extra one-dayers. Later we found out this was not very true because the Pakistan Board, in one of their correspondences, said that it would be difficult for them to play more cricket because of issues to do with logistics and security. So we went and by that time Ranatunga was replaced by a new Chairman of the Board and they had split the tour into two. So we went and played one-dayers and then we went for the Test matches. Driving in on the third day of the second Test in Lahore I think everyone was fed up with Test cricket at that time because the wickets were so flat.

We were getting 500, Pakistan was getting 600. One of our fast bowlers makes mention, you know, 'I hope there's a bomb because my back's going to give out bowling on these tracks so at least we can go home.' Thirty seconds later, carnage, you know. There's explosions, there's firing at the bus. Everyone hits the deck because from the front comes a shout saying they're shooting at the bus. So everyone's down on the deck and I think everyone remembers every second of it.

I don't think anyone relives it as a . . . as a horrible nightmare anymore. I think everyone's got a much better perspective of what happened now and emotionally they're in complete control when they live through it again whilst telling someone about it. It's funny the things that go through your mind and some of them are really funny. You know you are scared and you're expecting to be shot and you're also wondering who else is shot. And then you hear the bullets going through the bus and the groans coming down the aisle towards you and you're thinking okay one, two, maybe it's me next.

I think one of the reasons why we can look back, and I can even laugh at it at times, is that no one died [from the Sri Lankan team and match officials]. I think if we had lost a player or an official or a coach . . . our responses would have been very different. But I don't know, for some reason no one was killed; a few players were injured and Samaraweera quite badly. For us that was, I think, a moment. Where we live on the subcontinent sometimes you can get above yourself as a cricketer and think you are untouchable—you know, you are better, bigger than the game or anyone else even the fan. I think this put [it] into perspective [for us], understanding [that] like everyone else we can be touched, we can get killed, we can get shot at, we don't live charmed lives. I think it really brought [home] the reality of who we were and what we were supposed to do and that helped us get through it. The players recovered very quickly and were back playing cricket within months, within weeks. Samaraweera was back within a month and a half and scored a hundred, so I think emotionally we came to grips with it very well. But I think it will also scar us because I don't think our players would want to go back to Pakistan.

MAHELA JAYAWARDENE: It was a very sad moment, to be honest with you. At the same time, when you look back, we were prepared in a sense. I grew up in a war; when we were schooling we had our schools closed for weeks, for months because of violence, bombs in Colombo.

Or sometimes our parents wouldn't send us to school because there were threats on certain days and against certain people and certain activities. So we stayed at home. Even when we went to school they were scared that we would not come home in one piece. So we grew up in an environment like that for 25 years. Even when we were adults and playing for the national team you'd drive through Colombo and there was a good chance of a bomb going off at any given time. So if you're in the wrong place at the wrong time you'd be gone. So we grew up [with] that.

So when it happened we were very disappointed purely because beforehand we knew we were heading for trouble. There were threats and none of the other international teams were going. It was a decision that the Board took at that time. Whether it was political or not I don't know but I was disappointed as a captain and I was against it at the time. I wrote to them quite a few times but [we were] committed so we had to go. We were very thankful that nothing serious happened to any of our boys. It would have felt really bad if anything serious had happened to the team and things would have been [quite] different. Luckily for us everyone came through, with injuries, yes, but we were able to get them back on the playing field within four months and trying to play cricket.

It gave us a different perspective [on] our lives as well. It could have happened to anyone but to an international team in that situation was tough. But I think as a team we were able to handle the situation much better because we grew up in an environment like that as kids and it wasn't so traumatic that we needed a lot of help. I'm sure if it happened to some other countries, to some other players, it probably would be a much tougher ordeal to deal with. But for us I think the best thing that happened was that we were on the park playing cricket within a few weeks, three or four weeks, and the boys who were injured came back within a few months and we were all playing cricket together. So that was the best thing.

SIMON TAUFEL: To be honest, to cope I fell back on a lot of the training I'd done with Russell Trotter, my life skills coach. We'd done a lot of work on rational thought processes. Obviously it's a very emotional time and it's a very distressing time for yourself and the people around you and the people

[who] are closely connected to you. So no one can ever prepare you for something like that, you know. It's just one of those things out of the blue.

We actually stopped outside the ground and we had to run through the gate and into the umpires' room. In Lahore this umpires' room is sort of a bit like a dungeon in the bottom of the grandstand. Broadie [English match referee Chris Broad], Steve Davis [fellow Australian umpire], myself and Peter Manuel [the International Cricket Council's regional manager of Pakistani and Sri Lankan umpires] all sort of got in the umpires' room and without even looking at each other we sort of embraced each other and said 'How on earth did we get out of that?' My next thought was well, look, I need to ring my wife, Helen. I need to talk to her and there's no way I'm leaving this umpires' room for the next couple of hours. I don't care what anyone tells me. I'm surrounded by concrete and I'm now safe.

But then I started thinking a little bit later on that I needed to check on the players. So I went down to the Sri Lankan dressing-room and spoke with Murali [Muttiah Muralitharan] and Mahela Jayawardene and Kumar Sangakkara, people that you know. We're one cricket family and even though it's a job you see these people so often that you do develop relationships with them on a very arm's length level. So I went down to the players' dressing-room and spoke to those guys. They were all in a surprisingly positive mood even though some of their players had been injured. I suppose given their culture, their history of what's happening in Sri Lanka and Colombo, they're probably a bit more used to seeing that than I am. But still, it's a tragedy.

Then it was all about how can I deal with this rationally? You know coming back home to Australia to see my friends and family and work through that. I'm not afraid to say that on the plane in Dubai I sat in my seat and I did cry and I thought about the time when I would actually see Helen for the first time. I didn't want to show her that I was emotional. I didn't want to show her I was upset or that there was a problem so I actually went through that experience on the plane. Then by the time I got back to Australia I was able to deal with that in a way that was very calm, measured, rational because I thought I needed to show strength to Helen. Some people might disagree but that was the way I could handle it. I thought—okay we've been through a terrible event. Yes, it was nasty. Yes, people died. Yes, people sacrificed their lives for us and it was a terrible thing for cricket as well. But we got through it, we're alive, we can move on and we need to.

So it was a matter of dealing with it in a very matter-of-fact way and saying how best can we manage to go forward. If I'm going to stay involved in cricket what are we going to do now to safeguard us as much as possible? Obviously security's beefed up for the convoys, it's beefed up for the hotels, for transport between airports and grounds. Most of the places we go to now we have our dedicated security officer. This brings its own challenges because someone's walking with you at dinner. He might be carrying a firearm, he might not be. There are different threats no matter where you go. Some of them might be a terror threat, some of them might just be a personal safety threat because every place you go to is different. So it's a matter of doing your research, working closely with the administrators, looking at the security plans, being responsible for safety yourself. You know, don't open your door in a hotel to someone you don't know, all those sorts of things, making sure that the plan has been executed as agreed. You know there are guards on your floor, there are metal detectors at the front of the hotel, your car is searched for bombs before you get into the compound, you do present your bag for searching when you enter the ground, all those sorts of things. And you wear your accreditation pass so that everyone knows who you are. You have a responsibility to yourself and to other people to recognise that. Okay, cricket's changed and we have to adapt and we have to work within that environment. But life goes on.

The portents were discouraging for David Gower when he led his England party back to the Indian subcontinent late in 1984. Earlier in the year he had inherited the England leadership from an ailing Bob Willis against Pakistan in Faisalabad. And while he grasped the opportunity and became the first English captain to score a hundred since Tony Greig in India seven years earlier, he could not save England from their first series defeat at the hands of Pakistan.

But such was his form—a record 449 runs at 112.5 in Pakistan—that he officially succeeded Willis as captain for the home series against Clive Lloyd's formidable West Indian team and within two months suffered the ignominy of what the tabloids termed a 'blackwash'.

This was followed by a lacklustre draw against Sri Lanka at Lord's—England's record-equalling twelfth match without success.

While officially he was only months into his captaincy he did not need to be reminded by the remorseless English press that eight of the 12 matches had been on his watch. Intensifying the pressure was his knowledge that two of his three immediate predecessors had triumphed in India—Greig engineering a 3–1 success in 1976–77 and Mike Brearley overseeing a 10-wicket victory in a solitary Test in Bombay in February 1980 to celebrate the golden jubilee of the Board of Control for Cricket in India.

> **DAVID GOWER**: The summer of 85 was an absolute favourite for me. If anyone ever asks me about my best year well, that was it, the summer of 85—the runs as a batsman, to lead the England side to victory in an Ashes series, six matches, you know—three, four months' hard work. That was a pinnacle and it was important, I think, coming into that through the tour before—the tour of India which, is a testing tour, a long tour; four months. And very few England captains won in India so that in itself was special. I think that was important leading up to the Ashes series of 85 because in India there were so many things to deal with, extraordinary things to deal with. And it was good for me to have come through that and it was good for the team to have come through that—to learn from those experiences.

We arrive in India at the start of this four-month tour in the early hours of the morning—the same morning that Indira Gandhi is shot by one of her own bodyguards. And we do a press conference that morning where we say we'd like to offer our condolences to the Indian nation on the loss of their leader, of your leader. And the Indian journalists in that room had no idea because the news had gone from various embassies back to London, back to us. It wasn't . . . it hadn't been made known in India at that stage. So we've got a . . . we're revealing to the Indian journalists in that room that their prime minister, their premier, has been assassinated that morning. We then have to deal with the whole thing and take advice from our high commissioner in Delhi. We were advised we could stay in the country but we could do nothing for the two weeks of national mourning. So we went to Sri Lanka for two weeks. They very kindly offered us the chance to play some cricket and off we went.

We came back to India with the tour now back on, we got to Bombay [Mumbai] and we had a night out with our Deputy High Commissioner [Mr Percy Norris], a fabulous night out, great hospitality. It was just one of those real pleasures on tour—sometimes they can be stifling, sometimes a joy and that was a joy. The following morning he is assassinated in the streets of Bombay. You can imagine what it's like for a touring team. You know once is unlucky, you might say, twice you're starting to worry and again we're in the hands of a High Commission. And their advice? We were told this time, no, it's fine, don't be alarmed. The fact that people like

British Airways are closing down their offices in Bombay for the day and other British institutions, banks and stuff, were taking all possible precautions—it was alarming.

We got on with the job again. As captain and with my manager on that tour, Tony Brown, we had to talk to the players that morning. Firstly to break the news; and, you can imagine . . . I mean some of them . . . you know, the shock. Then we said: Right, we're in this together. So we had this whole couple of days where we had to basically draw people together, keep people together. And there were players who were firmly of the opinion that we should be on a plane heading out of there. We didn't, we stayed. We said, well, if you want to go you can go. But, you know, we pulled that back together and we played the Test match in Bombay. Sadly we lost that [by eight wickets]. I was on Keith Fletcher's tour three years previously where we'd lost the first Test match in Bombay and we had five of the most horrible draws, the most boring mind-numbing draws for the rest of that tour. I was fearful of that happening again.

So now we had a cricketing problem to sort out, which is a relief in many ways because you can then get people's minds firmly back on to cricket. I had a very good deputy on that tour in Mike Gatting. You know things that add up. The fact that I made Mike vice-captain gave him the fillip to actually get his career started, which is something he's always remarked on to me. I look back on that as a joy, too, because captaincy is about getting the best out of as many people as possible. And with Mike on that tour he made runs, he was a good deputy. It was all a part of that team coming together and when we'd finished that tour, won at Delhi [by eight wickets], won at Madras [now Chennai, by nine wickets] and finished the tour 2–1 ahead that was satisfying. In a sense it was more satisfying than winning the Ashes in the following summer because of all the issues that went on during that tour.

So to get through that and to come out with a united team at the end of it was as important as everything that happened in the summer of 85 in England. It was the springboard for the Ashes.

Ghoulish it may seem but pictures of players seriously injured by the ruthless deeds of the world's most menacing bowlers are among the game's most memorable and compelling images.

Only the foolhardy and those without knowledge of the game's history trivialise or understate the extent of physical courage required by batsmen to confront the relentlessly combative fast bowlers who have always populated the game.

Partisanship is forgotten and crowds fall deathly silent when a batsman is struck a severe blow. For old-timers thoughts immediately turn to former Indian captain Nari Contractor and New Zealand tailender Ewan Chatfield, who came close to death when knocked senseless in international matches in 1961–62 and 1974–75 respectively.

RICK McCOSKER: That image of my face swathed in bandages, to me, doesn't rate against, say, Victor Trumper's image, you know, lunging out to drive and Don Bradman's cover drive. Not quite the same . . . but, yes, I recall that moment. I knew Bob Willis was going to bowl a bouncer. I guess when you're an opening batsman you can generally read an opening bowler . . . fast bowler. They get that look in their eye as they're coming in to bowl so I had a pretty fair idea that it was going to be a bouncer. All sorts of thoughts . . . I mean it's amazing when you think back. I mean at the time it happens in a millisecond. Yet thoughts were going through my head at the time.

This is the first morning of the Centenary Test. Up there in the stand [are] some of the greatest players of all time including Sir Donald Bradman. So what would Don Bradman have done to that, to a bouncer at the MCG? He would have gone back on his back foot and he would have smashed it through . . . you know, in front of square leg for four. So, yep, I thought, well this is the Centenary Test, there's 70,000 people in the ground that's what I'll do. But it just wasn't the right shot and the right time.

And I broke an unwritten rule that you never play a hook shot on the MCG in the first session of a Test match because the bounce is uneven and the pace is uneven because of the moisture in the wicket. So, yes, I paid the price. I didn't know what damage had been done and the worst thing for me was that the ball fell on the stumps and just dislodged the bails. So the first thought that went through my mind was that I'm out. I didn't feel anything for a while because my whole face went numb. There were a couple of nerves that were broken and the whole face just went numb completely and then it started to swell up. So it wasn't until later in the morning that it was decided that I'd better go and have an x-ray because my face was up like a balloon. So then it was found out that my jaw was broken.

I spent that day in hospital and somebody had brought in a radio for me and I was listening to the ABC broadcast. It was agony just sort of hearing . . . you know all the rest of the guys were all out for a very low score [138]. So that didn't help much at all. But then, the next day I was still in there for a while and then listening to Dennis [Lillee] and Maxie Walker, you know, going through the Poms as well. So that sort of lifted the mood a little bit. I wanted to be a part of this huge occasion but couldn't because of what had happened. I was, I guess, very frustrated and disappointed that I couldn't be a part of it. I couldn't get out on the ground and field so I was very disappointed from that point of view.

But as we developed the second innings and the wicket really flattened out . . . it was a beautiful wicket and they had a very good batting side. So we knew that we had to give them a big target. Marshie [Rod Marsh] was getting close to his 100 and we wanted to make sure he got it. But secondly we needed more runs so I was ready to go in any time, really. Greg [captain Chappell] came and asked me did I want to bat and said the decision was mine. I said, well, okay, that's what I want to do. So Greg kept putting me back further and further and it got to the stage where the second new ball was about to be taken and Gary Gilmour got out. So Greg said I'll hold you back now because the new ball is just about due. So he asked Dennis Lillee. So I've never lived that down, an opening batsman being shielded from the new ball by a fast bowler. He's never let me live that one down. By the time I got out there it was drinks on the last session of the day and the England side had been in the field for a day and a bit and it was a flat wicket. The ball was starting to get old and, you know, batting was fairly easy. Yes, John Lever let me have it straightaway.

But it is Test cricket and you expect that. But the wicket was so flat and he was pretty tired so it was a fairly innocuous bouncer. It was just instinct, you know . . . it is there, this is what you do and that's just what I did. So it was exciting just to be out there and being a part of this match and hearing the crowd, and feeling the crowd, feeling the vibes from the crowd especially when Marshie got his 100. That was just great.

McCosker (25) helped Marsh (110 not out) add 54 for the ninth wicket. Australia won the match by 45 runs—astonishingly exactly the same margin of Australia's victory in the first Test match.

ANIL KUMBLE: There were a lot of instances in my career where I had come back and proved that I can deliver at the international level. So this was another opportunity for me to go out there and prove myself. It was all the emotions of the previous two or three Test matches—going into this Test knowing that I had not been a part of the playing eleven in the previous two matches. The first match I played, the second and third I was dropped so this was my real opportunity. So probably all these thoughts were there and then John Wright, the coach, came up to me and said I needed to bat one number ahead of Ajay Ratra, the wicketkeeper. You know people think that batting at number eight is pretty simple. But when you go in at number eight you have the second new ball always. So John Wright thought I could handle the second new ball slightly better than Ratra. So it was my duty to go up the order. I got hit but I continued because I was committed to staying there and not exposing Ratra. But after three overs I got out.

You know Antigua is not the ideal place to have a medical emergency. So I was diagnosed as not having a fracture. So that night I went into the gym, trained and then I was ready. I knew that I had to bowl the next day and we had 600 runs on the board. The following morning I knew something was wrong. I had a broken jaw. I knew that. So I went into the doctor, the specialist and he said: 'You have a broken jaw and you have to go back home to get it fixed at the earliest.' So I knew I was going back home and all these emotions—of not having played, getting this opportunity and getting hit and having to go home. Maybe all those emotions really helped me garner the courage and go out there and say: 'Look I can, I can get a wicket, my shoulder is fine.' I always believed that if my shoulder was fine I was fine.

So I just thought my shoulder's okay I'll go out there and bowl. But the physio didn't think that I could do that. He thought I was joking so I told him to strap me up and I would just go out there and bowl. That was probably what it was—the emotions leading up to the Test match and also what happened. You know those incidents probably helped me muster courage to go out there and bowl.

SACHIN TENDULKAR: There have been many special moments in life where it actually tests your character. It makes things difficult for you. And there have been some moments in which you anticipate certain things to happen and then everything falls into place and you move smoothly. But a defining moment in my life, without any doubt has to be on my first tour of Pakistan in 1989. We were playing a Test match in Sialkot and in the second innings were 38 for four and I was batting on two and I got hit on my nose by Waqar Younis. In that particular match there were only two players not wearing a grille—[Kris] Srikkanth, our captain, and me. So there was direct impact on my nose and I managed to stay there and we saved that game for India. After that it made me mentally tougher, very strong and I had an Australian tour, which was immediately after that. I felt terrific after that tour because I did reasonably well. So I thought that the Pakistan tour and the four Test matches were a defining moment because they changed me as a person. I thought that is fine now, if I get hit by a ball the damage can only be to this extent and nothing more is going to happen and I can deal with it. So it made me a different person.

Given his aristocratic lineage and thrilling precociousness as a batsman there was broad concern when Mansur Ali Khan, once the Nawab of Pataudi, seriously injured his right eye in a car accident in 1961, his second year as captain of Oxford University.

From his earliest days at Winchester College there was an expectation that he would, like his father, make the progression to English first-class cricket and subsequently to the Test match arena. His father, Iftikhar Ali Khan, Nawab of Pataudi, had the distinction of playing for both England and India and was a famously disenchanted member of Douglas Jardine's infamous Bodyline team to Australia in 1932–33.

Known to his teammates as Pat or 'Tiger', Pataudi, who had made his debut for Sussex in 1960, had amassed 1216 runs at 55.27 with four hundreds and was in reach of his father's record aggregate of 1307 when the accident happened at Hove in the county of Sussex.

Showing a steely resolve which was to characterise his future cricket, he returned to the nets as soon as was practicable and learned to adjust to batting with his right eye severely and permanently damaged.

So successful was his rehabilitation that just months later and 22 days before his 21st birthday he played his first Test match for India against England at the Feroz Shah Kotla ground in Delhi.

A natural leader of men with a deep and abiding love of India, Tiger captained India in 40 of his 46 Test matches including 11 against Australia.

The Nawab Mansur Ali of Pataudi assumed the name of Mansur Ali Khan after the Indian government abolished royal titles. Since 2007 the Pataudi Trophy has been awarded for Test match competition between India and England.

> **MANSUR ALI KHAN PATAUDI**: I had to find within myself determination and, perhaps, an ability to not get completely frustrated. To get over the fact that I could never be what I would have liked to have been. That I was, let's say, 30 or 40 per cent below what I would have liked to have been and to accept that. That took a while to do and took a bit of doing.

There has been no more beguiling cricketer than Wesley Winfield Hall, whose recorded and celebrated account of his last over in the tied Test match with Australia in Brisbane in December 1960 has long been regarded as classical cricket lore.

Considered close in pace to the game's fastest bowlers, Australian Jeff Thomson and Englishman Frank Tyson, Hall has led a rich life as a politician and preacher in the Pentecostal Church since his illustrious career as a cricketer.

Much loved in Australia where he played for Queensland from 1961 to 1963 and for the Randwick Grade Cricket Club in Sydney in 1966–67, he was never intimidated by his surroundings or those around him and never short of a word.

> **WES HALL**: You know, when you go to a country and that's 50 years ago [the West Indies renowned tour of Australia of 1960–61] I mean you . . . you look for your own. And that is exactly what I did especially in Brisbane. Even when I went back to Australia I had a lot of Aboriginal friends. I remember Jimmy Little the singer and Darby McCarthy the jockey. You really do look for your own and you look back at history. I once did a lecture at the University of Toowoomba and talked

about the Indians in Canada, the Indians in America, the Jews and all the castes, the African slavery in the Caribbean and, yes, the Aborigines of Australia. Yes, that is something that was very dear to my heart. As a matter of fact I once played in a prime minister's match in Canberra and Mr Menzies, he was the prime minister, came up to me and asked if I loved Australia. And I said: 'Oh, I really do love it.' And I was genuine. I really do love Australia and he asked me three times if there was anything at all that I didn't like and I said 'Oh, no, I do love the place.' And at the third time I said: 'Well, I'm not too amused by your White Australia Policy.' He said: 'Really!' And I said: 'Yes, because I don't understand how you could have me here because I can bowl a ball fast and my brother, who is a better character, a brighter man, couldn't come. So that is something that has me, you know, very bemused.' He said: 'Oh!' I must say the aftermath was although I got a lot of wickets in that game I didn't get invited again so I wasn't too popular for my honesty.

The *Wisden Cricketers' Almanack* of 2004 began its report of the 2003 World Cup semi-final between Australia and Sri Lanka this way.

'This was Gilchrist's match, not for what he did with bat or gloves but for his decision to walk, which astonished everyone unused to such Australian magnanimity.'

ADAM GILCHRIST: At that moment it was spontaneous; just a reaction to what had happened. I just stood up and clearly remember just looking at Rudi [umpire Koertzen] saying 'Not out'. But everything in my body just said go, walk, that's out. So I went. I didn't wake up that morning or had never woken up saying, agenda item number one: I've got to walk or make sure everyone walks or get on this crusade of being a walker and trying to change the mindset of those who don't. It's never been the case and still to this day I understand the intricacies of this game and the mindset of players. It's a personal decision.

I think it was the culmination of a variety of things. Not the least I just felt the players, as players we were very good whingers and complainers of umpiring standards and of things not going right. We were very quick to blame things, quick to blame but were happy to receive a good one. I just felt, as players, we could be a bit more accountable for our actions and, if we want, have an impact. That's probably where it got to me just trying in my humble way, one player in the history of cricket, trying to contribute. It's pretty unique I suppose, on reflection, that it all happens in a World Cup semi-final.

There was a moment when I didn't walk in a game when I was about 19 playing for the New South Wales Second XI or the Academy team against an ACT team where I smashed one on a low score off a spin bowler and didn't get out and went on to score 100. I felt so bad. I went to the bowler who was an ageing leg-spinner who'd been to Sydney and he'd tried his luck and was back now playing in Canberra. I said: Oh, mate, I'm so embarrassed about that, I'm sorry.' He said: 'No dramas, it obviously means a bit more to you than it does to me, so don't worry about it.' That remark just seemed to stay with me and I thought, hang on, does it have to mean that much to me that I now feel awkward about my actions. So maybe that was a bit of a defining moment—more than in 2003.

Everyone asks what happened back in the dressing-room. It wasn't what they said it was what they didn't say! The silence was deafening until Ricky Ponting said: 'Didn't you see him give you not out?' Ricky had gone in once I got out and I thought: Gee, have I done the right thing there? It'll be alright, Ricky will score a hundred and we'll be right. But he got out reasonably quickly and next thing he's sitting next to me and asking did I see the umpire give me not out. I said yes and that was the wrong answer, too. Look no, that's probably over-dramatising it. The guys were a little bit uncertain as to what had just happened.

But over time I never felt really uncomfortable. There were times through the rest of my career when I wondered whether things were being said but not to the point that it became an issue. I felt very well supported by Ricky as a captain. He was very clear and concise. Like I say, it's an individual choice. Did I walk through my career? Yes, I can't remember any other time that I didn't walk but I'll stand corrected if someone can come up with it. I don't remember times where I didn't. Maybe that semi-final was what drew attention to it and it got me thinking more about why I have this philosophy. But I don't remember begrudging anyone who didn't. Still don't. Just play it how you want to play it.

As about 1000 Europeans arrived in Australia with the First Fleet on 26 January 1788, members of the Marylebone Club which had been formed the previous year were revising the laws of cricket.

Indeed, the members of the club wrote the new code before a ball had been bowled on Thomas Lord's new ground, which is now invariably referred to as the spiritual home of cricket. First written in 1744, there were revisions to the laws in 1755, 1774 and 1786 before the 1788 redrafting at the direction of the 'The Cricket Club at St Mary-le-bone.'

For its bicentenary in 1987, Tony Lewis, a former England captain and renowned broadcaster who became president of the MCC, wrote an unconventional and eminently readable history of the club and cricket entitled *Double Century.*

In his preface he said: 'The Marylebone Club is still considered by some to be haughty and autocratic; many believe that a privileged, public-school style of posture still runs the cricket world as it did up to the Second World War.'

While he then cited personal experience to debunk the contention such a perception still exists in many quarters within England and far beyond. Former England captains Tony Greig and Rachael Heyhoe-Flint had good reason to believe they had encountered an intransigent autocracy when they dug in their heels on matters of principle that deeply affected them and their contemporaries.

TONY GREIG: It was very, very tough. I mean . . . look if it had not been for Kerry Packer I'm not sure I would have handled it very well. I would have been out of there . . . out of

England a lot earlier. Well, I mean, everything came tumbling down. They took the captaincy away from me, which was to be expected. I played and didn't play too badly, still played quite well in that series against Australia [1977] but it wasn't my team any more. You know, this was now Brearley's team and we had to move forward. And, of course, the plans for the winter weren't going to involve us because we were going to Australia. Yes, it was tough. You couldn't go anywhere without . . . you know, especially the establishment . . . I mean you go to Lord's and there would be very quiet treatment—letters, lots of letters from people like Jim Swanton [influential writer and author], people that I respected, you know, Alec Bedser. I had long discussions with him. He had been a great supporter of mine so that aspect of it was very hard, looking back at it now.

And also the pressure—I mean the last resort for me was when I went to pick up my daughter, my little girl from her school, the kindergarten in Brighton. They had a little tradition where on a Friday afternoon when you picked your little girl up, they had birthday parties on the Saturday, and they used to give the invitation to the parents. My little girl's best friend had a party on that Saturday. I was there to pick up Sam as our match must have finished early. My little girl did not get an invitation and her best friend came over and said, 'Have you got yours?' And she said 'No.' She ran across to her mother and said, 'Sam hasn't got her invitation.' And the mother looked at me and said: 'She's not invited.'

After that I went home and I picked the phone up to Kerry and said: 'Mate, I'm ready to move.' That was the July of '77. He said: 'Mate, don't do anything. Speak to my secretary. You'll be flying out, we'll pack the house up.' And that was it. I left. So yes, it was tough. It was a hell of a tough thing to do, pack your home up and leave, you know, and be happy to be going because of the pressure that was brought to bear.

Did I feel an outcast? I mean 'outcast' is a little bit heavy. I mean, I knew what I was letting myself in for. I knew that I was going down to Australia eventually but, you know, I was taken aback a bit by the fact that I thought these guys [the cricket establishment generally, and the Marylebone Cricket Club specifically] had got it so wrong. They didn't understand. I mean, they were almost adamant that they weren't going to try and see this from our side of the fence at all . . . it was totally one-sided. It was disappointing.

As time goes by and you see things happen, you start to look back and think we made a contribution. We bit the bullet—we did something that took a bit of courage to do. And, you know, that's why I feel a little bit sorry for one or two of the other blokes. I felt a bit sorry for them because a lot of them had followed me. You know, guys like Derek Underwood. He was given a hard time. Dennis Amiss had an incredibly tough time. Knotty [wicketkeeper Alan Knott], John Snow not quite so much because he was at the back end of his career. But I felt responsible for them so it's been a pleasure to see people like Derek Underwood become president of the MCC. The wheel has turned full circle.

It was easier to play the game we'd been trained to play from a little boy. So facing a fast bowler, you know, they start you out and eventually they get quicker and quicker and quicker as you go up the ladder. But to take on the establishment in England! There were things that happened. You've no idea the pressure. I'll give you an example. We decided to go after the best possible lawyers we could in the UK, and Slater and Mayer was the name of the company we went after but Lord's had already got them because, as you can imagine, most of these people at Slater and Mayer, these great lawyers, were MCC members. So we ended up with a company called Linklaters and Paines also, I mean, one of the top law firms, very establishment. All of them had their kids at Eton and Harrow. So we had our first meeting with them and Jock Harper was from Allen Allen & Hemsley here. He was our man who introduced us to this company. Kerry and I wanted to play golf that day so Kerry said to Jock 'Phone them up, tell them we'd like to go ahead with the meeting but we're playing golf. We've got the chopper picking us up at the Battersea Heliport.' So I had this other side of my life as well now. I had Packer and I had helicopters and, you know, going to golf. I hadn't had any of this stuff so I was quite impressed, I've got to tell you, with the exposure to the Packer way of life. But I certainly wasn't happy with the way he treated the establishment because I still had this very high regard of having to tiptoe through the tulips a little bit with them and try and massage them a little bit. So off we went. They served coffee in these little cups and, you know, it was all very English and they were all in striped suits and they were . . . Kerry, I thought, was quite rude to them. Basically he looked over at the spokesman and said: 'Right, this won't take long. Who's the best QC in the country?'

Well, this guy had his nose put out of joint because his answer was: 'Mr Packer, this is nothing like Australia, you know. We have many eminent men here capable of handling this for you. Why don't you just leave it to us! Yes, why don't you just leave it to us!'

And Kerry said: 'Mate, I don't think you understand.' Exactly like that, you know. 'Mate, I don't think you understand. Who is the best QC? I'm not asking you how good you are versus Australia, who's the best QC in this country?' He turned to Jock Harper and said: 'Jock, these guys don't understand how we work. Organise another meeting. We'll ask the same questions. We're going to play golf.'

And I'm thinking, Kerry, we won't end up even being able to get a lawyer to work for us. And I said this to him and he said, 'Don't worry, wait until tomorrow.' We go back the next day and this time we've got suits. And back we go and there's a new spokesman and Kerry says: 'Remember the question.' I mean seriously rude, remember the question.

'Mr Packer, we've narrowed the field to three. Right, there is Mr Robert Alexander who we think is the best cross-examination man, not just in this country, the world.'

'Right, we'll have him,' says Kerry.

'Oh, it's not that easy, Mr Alexander is very expensive.'

Kerry at this stage, is you know: 'Give me his number.' Well, he's down in the Gulf on an oil case . . . 'Well, if you can't get him just give me his number.' I think Kerry had plans of incentivising him, or whatever, I don't know. They were happy and wanted to leave and Kerry said: 'Who are the other two?' There's so and so who's an all-rounder and there's Andrew Merritt who is the best point of law man in this field.

'We'll have him as well,' said Kerry.

These guys were [thinking] 'Hang on, these chaps are very expensive and you want two. It's unheard of two men of this standing. There won't be room for anyone else in the court because, you know, they have people behind them.' So we eventually got Robert Alexander and we got Andrew Merritt and we won the court case.

But I've got to say in the early days I thought Kerry's handling of the establishment was just over the top. But he had this way of, you know, getting what he wanted. In this case he did and [he got] those two guys because [they were] great friends and they came down to Australia. I think the incentive was if you win the case I'll give you the best holiday you've ever had in your life. And apart from getting paid a fortune they ended up coming down to Australia and falling in love with this place. And, of course, Robert Alexander went on to be the president of the MCC and Andrew Merritt was just as highly regarded. They were just brilliant.

RACHAEL HEYHOE-FLINT: I was rung one day by a reporter from the *Daily Mail* saying: 'I hear you've become a member of the MCC.' She was sitting at Lord's watching some cricket with her boyfriend.

I said: 'Well, no, I'm not allowed to be a member, I'm a woman, you know and it's an all male club.'

And she said: 'Well, why don't you join?' I said I thought that sounded like a good idea. So I wrote off my application form and then filled it in with my four sponsors: Tim Rice [now Sir Tim the lyricist and impresario], Dennis Amiss, the senior Warwickshire opener, Sir Jack Hayward, the British philanthropist who'd given money to the first indoor school and dear old Brian Johnston [renowned cricket broadcaster]. I thought that's a pretty good line-up. You had to have four supporters in those days.

I sent it off and then got a phone call from the then president Billy Griffith who said: 'We've never had an application from a woman before.'

I said: 'Oh!'

And he said: 'Well, I suppose we ought to address the problem, shouldn't we?'

And I said: 'Well, yes, I think you probably should,' and had a little laugh.

To cut a long story short, a nine-year story short, it took two annual general meetings, two special general meetings over a period of nine years. Each time a new president came in I'd drop them a note and say do you think the committee could possibly consider it. They had to change the whole constitution because by implication and by definition a member was a he and not a she, a man not a woman. So, you know, to change the mind and thinking of 18,000 members, all male, who loved the sanctity and the peace was quite . . . well it was time consuming. But we eventually did it. The one great supporter in that was Colin Ingleby-Mackenzie [MCC president 1996–98]. When he became president it was actually a two-year span at that stage. Whereas other presidents would only be in a year and it would be easy for them to drift along and, sort of cast me off into the background. But Colin Ingleby-Mackenzie was determined to drive it through. People said to him, why? And he said: 'Well, I love women and I love cricket and, you know what, what better than to have them as our members. And I think it is time that it is done.' Lo and behold we did eventually get the two-thirds majority but 4500 did actually vote against. And I've got to know who one or two of those are because when I walk into the Long Room, they sort of turn their back on me and don't buy me a drink, which is a shame really.

The one thing that would have alienated all the MCC members and the committee would have been if I'd taken a feminist stance, in other words demanded to be members because we are women. For such a prestigious club, as with any all-male organisation, you have to become part of the club ethos and philosophy and be a member. Not 'I am a woman therefore I demand to queue jump.' I think it's been that attitude that has gained me friends. And all the women who are members treat the whole place with due respect. As I say, I wouldn't want to join a flower-arranging club or a cookery club because I'm just not interested in that sort of thing. But

I love and adore cricket as do all the other women members and the men there obviously appreciate the women are there because of the love of the game of cricket. I only wanted to join because it was a cricket club, the greatest cricket club in the world and I just wanted to be a part of it. My whole life has been cricket.

The main thing was that we behaved as members. We didn't say: 'I am a woman therefore I demand certain rights.' Exactly the same stipulations relate—it's 18 years before you can become a member. You can become an associate member or playing member, which is a sort of fast-track. But it's full of the diehards who hate it: 'Oh, God, they'll be knitting and chattering in the pavilion. The whole place will change.' But it doesn't and I've heard a lot of chattering going on from the men there. After 10 years, 11 years, there was still, at that stage, only 600 or so members and not all those were full members. So there's no stampede of women coming in and pinching all the seats or anything. We behave in the best possible taste. I've been lucky because I've been included on various committees, the marketing committee as it was, the cricket committee. And I've been on the general committee twice and [am] about to become a trustee.

The international cricket community had scarcely digested the banning of Zimbabwean fast bowler Henry Olonga for an illegal bowling action when unconventional Sri Lankan off-spinner Muttiah Muralitharan was accused of throwing by Australian umpire Darrell Hair.

That Olonga and Muralitharan transgressed within 35 Test matches in 1995 was remarkable given that 32 years and 772 Test matches had passed since the dramatic ousting of Australian left-arm fast bowler Ian Meckiff by umpire Colin Egar at a Test match against South Africa in Brisbane.

Muralitharan, a wide-eyed, jovial Tamil from Kandy in the verdant hill country of Sri Lanka, polarised players, administrators, critics and spectators the world over and eventually compelled the game's legislators to tweak the laws and permit bowlers a 15-degree flex of the arm at the point of delivery.

He was disparaged as often as he was lauded and at times libelled and slandered yet somehow generally managed to maintain an impressive equilibrium as he became the world's greatest wicket-taker in both Test cricket and limited-over internationals.

> **MUTTIAH MURALITHARAN**: I didn't realise there could be some question about the legitimacy of my action until they called me. Some people are for me and some people are not for me. You can't change the world because some people think differently so you just have to go with the flow. And you have to produce all these tests and show that you are not doing wrong. So if you prove everything is right there's no problem. When I was young it was easier because others were defending me—especially [captain Arjuna] Ranatunga and the vice-captain Aravinda [de Silva] and the Cricket Board. And all the public of Sri Lanka was supporting me so that gave me strength not to give up. So from that I learnt you keep on and don't give up and just go through the process.

I went through the process and just proved myself that I'm not doing anything wrong.

Everyone can have an opinion. The laws of cricket had been that an umpire's opinion is the last opinion. And that was wrong at the time. You can definitely call a person for not bowling properly or chucking or whatever and you can destroy his career. And destroy him as well. So it is a big, big power they are given. So the ICC has taken all that power and said you have to prove if you're suspect and you have to go for a test. And then only the ICC with the technology available they will see whether he is good or not.

That has been introduced so I think that's a good introduction for cricketers and future cricketers as well. I think it's fair now. It was not fair before because I heard some people had been called for chucking but they couldn't prove anything. Nothing was done and their career was gone. They were not seen at all. See the 15 degrees is not huge—your naked eye can't see that moment. After 15 degrees the naked eye can see so that means you take advantage. So when they tested me my off-spin bowling was perfectly alright—about 10 degrees. Then they checked all the bowlers in the world in match conditions in ICC World Twenty20 and ICC 50-over games. It became well known the bigger bowlers come in more than 10 degrees. They didn't want to mention at the time that [Glenn] McGrath looks perfect and he came in more than 10 degrees. Brett Lee was like that as well and even Andrew Flintoff, who looked to have a perfect action was more than 11 degrees. The technology is so good they can measure inch by inch. Some people don't know about the scientific test. I think the ICC should make a study on that and see how all the professionals have done it. They use technology for everything so it's easy to use technology for bowling actions as well. Then you will know that someone has done wrong because technology has called out rather than the naked eye. No bowler is taking any advantage before 15 degrees and should be allowed. After 15 degrees it is an advantage for the bowler so that's why they then ban [them].

Statistically Australia's greatest opening batsman, Matthew Hayden ritually assumed the Zen position on match eve to visualise those who would oppose him and have the temerity to question his superiority: 'I was in a space which elevated my mindset to a gladiatorial position.'

CHAPTER FIVE

Philosophy

The power of one

Technology and the sports sciences have irrevocably changed the game. The science of cricket has become a highly specialised field of endeavour with its practitioners gaining a public profile and considerable influence in areas once the preserve of cricket experts.

As a consequence attitudes, perceptions, methods of operation and much more change constantly as the game in its various forms mutates. Even the language of the game is conspicuously different as the second decade of the 21st century gathers pace.

What does not change and will not change is each individual's quest for satisfaction, improvement, inclusion, promotion, recognition and success.

Many players have a personal philosophy. They may not couch it in this manner but they have a belief, a conviction, a credo, an instinct—something they believe will propel them forward and so set them apart.

The philosophy can be homespun and uncomplicated or grand and ideological. Often it will be informed by history—personal, family even country, race or religion. Sometimes it will be shared, at other times jealously guarded.

It might not amount to anything more than wanting to win at all costs. Conversely it could be about loftier matters—about purity of endeavour, joyful expression, obligation, wanting to right wrongs, setting standards, leading by example, making a difference. It could be about identity, equality, legacy, hope, tolerance and social responsibility.

Clive Lloyd, the distinguished West Indian captain who was created an honorary officer of the Order of Australia and twice decorated by the government of his native Guyana, believes fervently cricketers have the capacity to make the world a better place. Inspirational Sri Lankan captain Mahela Jayawardene agrees wholeheartedly.

Whether the picture is large or small, the unwritten, the unsaid and often unacknowledged personal philosophy is a compelling force.

Making a difference

MAHELA JAYAWARDENE: To have your own identity is very, very important. To be a free soul but work really hard for your success, which is the most important thing. Even if you're a naturally gifted player you will have to work at it and be better and better. You're only going to do it for a period of time so give it everything you've got and be a better human being, a better person and leave a legacy. Help others if you can. You don't have to do it in a big way, even a little way would make a huge difference. That has been my philosophy on and off the field so try and help people and live a better life. As simple as that. I mean it's not so complicated. It's a very simple philosophy. The game has given me a lot but even if you're not a cricketer as in just the normal person you should have a social responsibility in your own little way. I mean if you can afford you should help others because I think it's the way forward. I mean, you get a peace of mind. As a cricketer you have more opportunities. I try and use personality and those tools to help other people.

I'm doing various projects now in the north and east of the country. We've been raising funds for cancer hospitals and I'm trying to get school children involved in playing cricket in rural areas where they don't have opportunities. I'm giving them equipment to start playing cricket because I know what cricket has given me and I'm ever so grateful for that. So if I can change the lives of these kids who are underprivileged. I don't want them to play for Sri Lanka. I just want them to enjoy the game of cricket. It's as simple as that. For while they are playing cricket they'll learn something in their life, something that might change their life. So just in a little way trying to help somebody makes a huge difference. I've been brought up in that way and I will try and bring up my kids on the same path.

When cricket spells hope

KUMAR SANGAKKARA: I think cricket has always been above petty politics in Sri Lanka. It's been above racism, it's been above war; 30 years of war and everything's forgotten when there's a cricket match on. There was even talk of the LTTE [Liberation Tigers of Tamil Eelam] asking for a ceasefire in the 1996 World Cup final. There is a great social bonding over this sport and more so in Sri Lanka than anywhere else because of the tough times the country was going through.

Also, cricket represented an ideal state. No matter where you came from cricket was represented by every ethnicity every religion in Sri Lanka and everyone was equal. And for 30 years that is what our country was striving for on the battlefield. While that was going on there seemed to be this little bubble where cricket was played and it couldn't be touched by anything—not even exploding bombs and teams leaving Sri Lanka because of bomb explosions, which happened with some of the New Zealanders. For crowds at a cricket game and for the cricketers themselves over those six hours, five days, it was as if life was back to normal. As long as cricket was played there was hope and people would always flock to a game. They loved the game a lot more because I think for them it meant that there was hope. And that there was life, life worth living no matter how tough things got and that the country could come together and will come together in the ideal manner that they saw on the field.

I think we played quite an English brand of cricket up until the early 1990s. We were textbook-driven cricketers. We conducted ourselves in the old English manner. We were expected to subdue our natural flair and to conform. But I think that changed in the 90s and we had unorthodoxy being accepted and being celebrated. Suddenly with Muttiah Muralitharan, Sananth Jayasuriya, Aravinda de Silva and Arjuna Ranatunga playing a very Sri Lankan brand of cricket we broke those colonial shackles even in our cricket. We graduated from there to playing a brand of cricket that anyone watching us will instantly recognise as being Sri Lankan. I think that is the greatest legacy that the '96 team left us. They finally showed us what Sri Lankan cricket is and how beautiful and how wonderful it was to watch and also to play.

When I started I played cricket at home and was pushed by my father. I still am pushed by my father! My father always said you can't play a sport without knowing its culture and its history. He said that was the first step to understanding technique and the playing of the game. You can't do it just practising, hitting a ball. You've got to know what other people have done and how they have done it. I always had to read something of the game—*The Art of Cricket* by Don Bradman and *Batsmanship* by C.B. Fry. You know, on a tour of England I was playing at Lord's and Charles Fry—I think he was chairman of the MCC at the time—was talking to me. I said: 'You know, my father always said the best book to read about batting is by Charles Fry.'

He said: 'Well a lot of people think so,' and asked me what I was doing the next day. I said we were training at Lord's and he said he would come by and have a word with me.

And he comes in and he's carrying a book, gives it to me and said: 'This is a second edition copy of my grandfather's book and it's for you because you said that your father asked you to read this.' That was amazing, for Charles Fry to actually take the time to do that just because I said that it was the best book I was asked to read. Those experiences you can't have anywhere else. So my interest in Test cricket, my place in Test cricket, where I wanted to be and how many runs I wanted to get as a minimum in any form of the game, all this I think is definitely due to my father.

Life and death

WASIM AKRAM: I picked up when I was married when I was 25. My wife [Huma, who died aged 42 in 2009] was a psychologist and hypnotherapist from University College London and she used to help me around. She used to put me to sleep before a big game and remind me of performances. The whole routine took 10 to 15 minutes just to remind me what I wanted to do before the game. That actually helped me a lot. It was visualisation like the golfers do before a big tournament. I think nowadays cricketers are doing it as well.

Also what helped a lot was county cricket when I was 22 or 23. I enjoyed playing county cricket and spending time with those guys. Being a Pakistani and living in Lancashire with all the foreign culture and the foreign players. They were very welcoming and I improved as a person. I got confidence and when you're a confident person obviously the confidence oozes out of you as a professional and that's what happened to me.

I used to love playing against India. It's a different pressure altogether because of the history, the politics and the attention you get when you do well. I can imagine the Ashes is a massive tour but you know back home your driver, your dad, your mum, your in-laws, your uncles, you get out of your house and the people on the street are all saying 'You must win, you must win.' It's a matter of life and death.

That sort of pressure is totally different but it is fun as well. I got told if I performed in Australia I'd be recognised worldwide as a cricketer. I agree with that still today. My aim was always to perform well against Australia because I knew if I did well every team would follow automatically.

Broomstick and marbles

BRIAN LARA: Being an entertainer underpinned my philosophy as a batsman. There were times when you needed to grind out an innings and there were times the team needed you to bat and not worry about runs or anything—just bat time. But obviously on most occasions when people walk into a cricket ground they want to be entertained. And I felt I had good players around me who would hold up an end and do exactly what the team wanted and I could go out and express myself. You know, I had Jimmy Adams on occasions and I loved batting with Jimmy. I loved batting with Shivnarine Chanderpaul—these guys who don't challenge for that stage. They allow you to grow into your innings, into yourself and they play a supporting role while picking up a century as well. So obviously, having a fan base, you have to keep these people entertained—the ones who would tell you 'I'm coming to see you bat' or say 'I'm only going if Brian is batting'. On occasions you couldn't because of the situation of the match.

I'm very much a reactive player. I don't set out and say I'm going to bat this way or that. It doesn't matter if it's a boofhead bowling or whatever the case may be. I'm somebody who knows exactly how to go about my innings. You know you just can't go out and hit every single ball but obviously if there is something right there for you to go at, you need to go at it, you need to stamp your authority very early.

I came from a cricketing family and the first bat I had was a coconut branch shaved with a handle in it and a softball or an orange. I had six bigger (and older) brothers who all loved cricket. I mean for me to get an opportunity in the streets I had to get all six of them out to get an opportunity to bat sometimes with a broomstick.

It was just a matter of taking the stick out of the broom and breaking it in two and, you know, picking a marble, or an orange or lime and bowling so it comes back into you to play. So I could play a match by myself. Or if my brothers were around we would pick up anything we could put our hands on and play. Even later on in my career they made a cricket bat that was very slim and you would go out and hit a cricket ball. You'd know that if you were hitting it well in the middle that something the size of a proper bat would be much easier. So I saw the importance of the broomstick and stump and all of those things later on in my career. Obviously I believe that from very early I knew that cricket was definitely in my bloodline and my dad [Monty] was definitely focused on getting his kids playing cricket and ensuring that somebody made something of it.

Black pride

VIV RICHARDS: I was always, from a very young man, pretty tenacious about competing and in competition you've got to hold your chest up, I believe, be proud of what you're doing. The most important thing is to be confident in yourself. Basically, I try to have that and I backed myself and believed in what I had. I guess there were times when it goes through your mind that, 'Wow, I'm in a battle here.' You've got to compose yourself at times for you lose battles. But I was thinking the times you lose battles also prepares you [for] when you win the war. And the war was what I always wanted to win.

A lot of folks would say that I was the most arrogant bastard or whatever. Yes, I wouldn't mind that a bit because I was proud about the ability which I think God gave to me.

It was all about your presence so see how much that talent shines. I have seen in sport that it isn't all about the talent that you have. It's imposing the presence, the confidence you portray. These are some of the little things that at times I was blessed with. And I was happy to take that into battle because I was confident in whatever I was doing. And proud about it.

There are folks who say 'You are such an arrogant bloke' but I've always looked at it this way. Who are you representing? And it's not just your colour but folks, you know, who have never had the opportunities to do certain things. So there's the inspirational factor. So if you are confident about what you are doing why not have a little strut about it? That to me is pretty simple. A lot of people say 'Wow, I loved the way you went out there.' People still remember today. And it's not just people of your own culture, your own race but people from all walks of life. Whether it is a club cricketer, grade two or three or whatever, they tell you these things that they tried to take into a game so you were an inspiration in so many different ways to so many different folks. I felt 'Yes', I wouldn't mind being called a little cult figure. Not in the same mode as Elvis, but in your own little way, I was very much happy with that. We all have our own style and I think everyone should be quite proud about their style.

I was proud to be associated with the great name of Sir Donald Bradman, a figure who was revered. I'm happy for my name to be mentioned and folks speaking about me being the black Bradman but I would never have been able to have achieved the things he did. I'm lucky to be mentioned with the great man. Who wouldn't? And in my modest way I'm very privileged if someone mentions Vivian Richards, wow, the black Bradman. That is something that I am comfortable with because if I perceive the thinking, yes, I would be totally happy with that.

Power of change

CLIVE LLOYD: As sportsmen, cricketers have to show the world that it's a better place, a peaceful place to live in. Obviously you'll have racism but should we allow that to overshadow how [we] feel about things? I really think that sportsmen have a chance of changing how the world thinks; how peoples in the world think about one another. I think it's a better place when you mix and you understand the other side of the person. In the old days we didn't mix as much.

We went to Australia every eight years. Now we've been there more often they know more about us and we know more about them. A lot more people have travelled to watch Australia play in the West Indies and India and Pakistan and so on. So really and truly we have a great part to play in making the world a better place and I hope that during our period we managed to do so.

I have no time for racism. It is there but it would never cloud my judgement about things and people and the way they react. I never look at anything in just black and white. You always think before you make statements as there might be other elements to what has happened.

In the name of the father

SIR RICHARD HADLEE: It is a privilege to represent your country and it is something you should appreciate and respect. There are traditions and there are values. I'll never forget what Dad [renowned New Zealand captain Walter Hadlee] said to me as he said to my four brothers. 'Look, whatever you do take pride in your performance, do it to the best of your ability. Even if somebody does it better you can only give 100 per cent and if you do that no one can criticise your performance and your commitment to the game.' So these little things became quite powerful and inspirational. Dad always offered encouragement to learn about the history of the game.

Fundamental principles

JOHN WRIGHT: I feel that you have to have some fundamentals in place to be a great sportsman in any code. You have to have great skill, you have to have a technique that will stand up in any game at any stage and you have to be able to replicate that and be consistent. You have the make-up or create that mental environment that allows you to go out and apply yourself to the role that you perform for your team consistently day after day.

The greatest players have a huge desire, a huge want. And the other thing is that they love—they love what they do, they love batting, they love cricket. Working with a [Sachin] Tendulkar, for instance; I don't think he ever lost the joy of actually going out to bat. A [Rahul] Dravid, for instance, is a fantastic coach. He is his own coach who you help along the way. So there are fundamental qualities that will stand the test of time and there will be different flavours of cricket, different forms of it. Goodness knows we might have a T10 shortly. But you will need some of those basic skills and those basic sound values to excel. I grew up on a farm and my father always said you could lead a horse to water but you can't make it drink. And you can't coach want.

I've always felt a coach can help but he can only do so much. The players you really want to be working with and encouraging just want to get out there. They're going to get there come hell or high water. That's what you are looking for. That real desire that's in a player to make him a better player. And that has to come from within the player himself. The greatest players I've worked with have the greatest desire to be a champion batsman, a champion bowler.

I never played cricket until I was 12 because there wasn't a local team but my brothers and sisters say I talked about wanting to play for New Zealand from a very, very early age but I can't even remember that. I suppose over the years I've always had to prove myself. I've always enjoyed competition and the thing I miss about playing is not being in the middle and competing. I like competition and I like the challenge of proving to myself particularly that I can be a good coach.

Undying passion

GREG CHAPPELL: From my point of view what I loved about the game was the contest—you know, pitting myself against the opposition and preferably against the best the other team had to offer. To walk off at the end of the day, not necessarily with runs—preferably with runs as a batter—but with the knowledge that I didn't beat myself but that I'd actually forced the opposition to beat me. I think that was the great challenge for me and what I loved about the playing side of it.

I'm grateful that I've had other opportunities in other areas and I think the education, the mentoring side of it, is probably the next part I've most enjoyed outside playing. But I've enjoyed all of it and having the chance to have some input into the ongoing health of the game.

We grew up with our father encouraging us to play the game attackingly with a view to winning the contest. I fell in love with it very early and I'm still in love with the game. I'm still passionate about the game. Most of my waking and sleeping thoughts, even now, seem to be around the game of cricket. I mean I grew up as the grandson of Vic Richardson and then became the brother of Ian Chappell. I made the comment after my first Test hundred that perhaps I'll be recognised as Greg Chappell.

It was said with some jest but it was obviously something that I did feel. I wanted to break out and be my own person. But the scrutiny never really worried me. It was more about me worrying about what I had to do to be successful and focusing on those things that were more important. There were periods where it was perhaps a bit of a nuisance being interrupted by something external because of who you were. But to be honest I'm grateful for the fact I've had the opportunity to be recognised for having played the game of cricket. It's been more good than bad—I can tell you that.

Living in the moment

STEVE WAUGH: I think if you saw me in the first five or six years you'd say I was probably mentally weak as a player. I think I developed the mental toughness to survive really. Maybe it was always within me and I didn't know it. It is acquired through disappointment and failure and adversity. I think that's what builds up your mental toughness and then you sort of finetune it by having the strength not to give in to yourself—to do the extra yard at training and not take the soft option.

I think I acquired mental toughness playing for Bankstown. I didn't get any benefit scoring runs for Bankstown but it was tougher because people expected me to. It was hard to get up sometimes as there wasn't a crowd there, wasn't television and there wasn't the adulation you get. But I still prided myself on trying to score hundreds every time I played for Bankstown. You know mental toughness can be going to the nets and getting 20 throwdowns and making sure you hit every ball as well as you can. Not saying, I'll hit 15 good ones and it doesn't matter about the other five.

Towards the end of my career I started to do a bit more fitness work myself. I remember one time I was doing a lot of sprinting. I think it was 50-metre sprints and I had to do 20 laps of back and forward. I got close to 20 and I thought have I done 21 or 19? I thought to myself, okay, I'd better do one more to make sure it is 20. And that was the signal to me that I was ready to keep playing because I could have said, no, I've done 21 and walked off. But I wasn't sure I'd done 21 and I made sure I did one more to make doubly sure I'd done 20.

So little things like that give you mental toughness and it is something you can acquire and something you can practise. I think Justin Langer said it one time that you can only think of one thing at a time when you're batting. If you think about two things you are in trouble. So it's got to be purely on what you're doing right now. I think that was the philosophy I took into cricket: that you do the best you can on this ball right now coming at you.

Tough love

NEIL HARVEY: During the Second World War we had to make our own fun. We didn't have any ovals close to us to play cricket but alongside our house there was a cobblestone back lane. That was our cricket pitch. On Sundays when the six boys were home we used to play 'Test' matches on the cobblestone back lane. Of course, you can't play with a cricket ball, which we didn't have anyway, and we used to make our own bat out of a piece of wood. So we used to play with a

The Man: unhelmeted, as was his wont, Viv Richards pulls with characteristic power and belligerence ahead of square. An indomitable and charismatic figure, he played for his people and culture and was proud to be called the Black Bradman.

Always the entertainer, Shane Warne made a smooth transition from artist to critic. Arguably the greatest leg-spinner in the annals of the game, his maverick nature obscured the fact he was a cerebral cricketer and a brilliant if unfulfilled captain.

One of only three English captains to have led in 50 Test matches, Andrew Strauss provided stability while respecting the individual flair of his teammates.

English batsman Mike Atherton made his Test debut in 1989 and was immediately confronted by irascible Australian fast bowler Merv Hughes. 'You got a gob-full after every ball, that's how it was,' said Atherton.

Maestros and mates, Shane Warne and Brian Lara pose with the Frank Worrell Trophy, which Sir Donald Bradman instituted for competition between Australia and the West Indies after the unforgettable tied Test series of 1960–61.

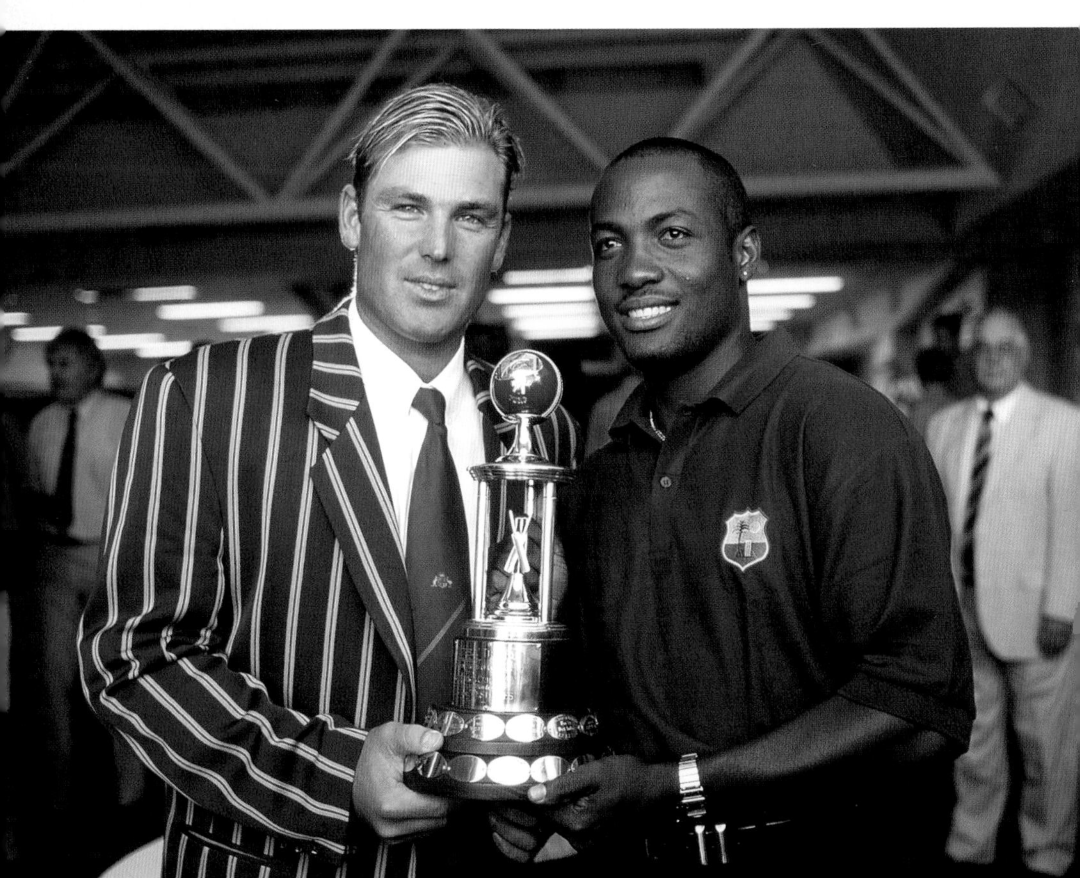

Adam Gilchrist acknowledges the ovation after another command performance.

Peerless left-arm fast bowler Wasim Akram with another addition to the trophy cabinet.

Cricket royalty: New Zealand's third captain, Walter Hadlee, with his renowned son Richard, who captured 431 Test wickets at a miserly 22.

There has been no more beautiful or poetic a sight in cricket than the incomparable Michael Holding, he of the mellifluous voice of commentary, working from his full run.

To the unbridled delight of coach Gary Kirsten, the longest-serving captain in Test history, Graeme Smith, carries the International Cricket Council's orb signifying South Africa's world supremacy in 2012. The hastily written sentiment on his shirt is a respectful nod to veteran wicketkeeper Mark Boucher, who retired following a serious eye injury.

England captain David Gower enjoys the saying ascribed to Napoleon: 'In victory you deserve champagne, in defeat, you need it.' Gower deserved it in 1985 but needed it in 1989 when his counterpart Allan Border triumphed in the return Ashes bout.

Courageous England captain Mike Atherton became the most celebrated target of provocative if guileful Australian paceman Glenn McGrath. To his despair, Atherton fell to McGrath a world record 19 times in the 66 innings he played against Australia.

Another headache for redoubtable New Zealand stalwart and captain, Daniel Vettori.

Indian batsman Rahul Dravid delivering the Sir Donald Bradman oration at the Australian War Memorial, Canberra, in 2011.

Englishmen abroad: the contemporary voice of English cricket, Jonathan Agnew (right) with former England captain Michael Vaughan on radio duty in South Africa.

The insurrectionists: media tycoon Kerry Packer and former England captain Tony Greig find occasion to smile during the nerve-racking weeks in advance of the first season of World Series Cricket in 1977–78.

Unforgettable: incomparable Dennis Lillee hails his dismissal of Viv Richards for 2 on the last ball of play at the Melbourne Cricket Ground on Boxing Day, 1981. Lillee finished with match figures of 10–127 and overhauled the world record of 309 Test wickets held by West Indian off-spinner Lance Gibbs. The spoils also gave him a then record 85 wickets for the calendar year.

tennis ball and we used to wet [it] in a bucket of water down at the bowler's end so it would slide off the cobblestones a bit quicker. And, of course, there's a groove between the cobblestones and it would either go one way or the other. It was a good grounding area.

When all of us weren't there two of us would go around to a tree around the corner. The trees had guards around them and the guards used to serve as a wicket. We'd play cricket in the street and we used to teach ourselves how to play. And that's how it was until we started to grow a little older and we could all join the Fitzroy Cricket Club. I think if you're brought up the hard way in a lowish-class suburb and get no favours from anybody you get a little bit of toughness that proves you can handle most things later on in life.

Knowing yourself

GLENN McGRATH: I never wanted to walk on to the field feeling under-prepared so I always did the hard work whether that was in the gym or in the nets. There was always that preparation. I remember the story when someone said to Gary Player that they wished they could hit a golf ball like him. 'Well if you go and hit 1000 balls a day you will,' Player said. So it's putting the time into it and knowing yourself and knowing your game well.

I was never a big swinger of the ball. I didn't bowl a big outswinger. My strengths were hitting the deck, getting bounce, a little bit of movement and accuracy and I always felt confident I could fall back on that and rely on that no matter what was happening or how I was feeling. The days I did try to bowl quick or did try to swing it I lost that bounce.

Talking to guys like Brian Lara and Sachin Tendulkar they said it was always tougher to face a guy who got more bounce whether he bowled at 130 or whatever rather than a guy who bowled at 150 plus who really skidded the ball on. So that, I guess, was just trial and error throughout my career. In my early days I tried to swing the ball as I was listening to guys who said to succeed at Test cricket you've got to be able to bowl a consistent outswinger. So I started bowling an outswinger but it wasn't very consistent. Then I got dropped from the team and it made me think I got picked for a reason and I should go back to that, work on it and improve as much as I could while looking to add a few other things to the armoury. I guess accuracy, bounce and consistency were probably my forte.

I always had a bit of fun and games with batsmen. I always said you never have to out-think a batsman because they're not that smart anyway. It's two totally different forms of the game. I think being a batsman is very reactive and being a bowler is pro-active. That's why I always felt that a bowler can use that to his benefit. I guess I thought I could use the media and come out and target a batsman I wanted to get out and say this is how I'm going to get him out. If I got him then the media would do the rest. I guess I was always secure within myself to feel that if he was good enough to beat me at my own game then so be it. If he hits me for a few balls then I've always got the next ball to bowl. And it only takes one ball. If a batsman makes a bit of noise in the media saying he is going to do this or that to a bowler he's on a bit of a hiding to nothing.

So that was the advantage of being a bowler and how we could benefit by having a bit of a chat before the game even started. So, yes, you know batsmen seem to think they're the most important ones in the game. Obviously, I think the bowlers!

Towards the end of my career I started to get a bit more feedback from a few different guys within the team. And some of them liked it and some of them didn't like it. I think in the end it was just a given that this is what I would do or Warnie [Shane Warne] or someone else would do and they just accepted it. I think Ricky [Ponting] maybe cringed every time I made a prediction or targeted a batsman. But looking back when I targeted a batsman it was actually quite successful. Probably 95 per cent of the time it worked in my favour. I was always focused on what we had to do in the middle to be successful and to win.

Zen in the middle

MATTHEW HAYDEN: To me there are so many things that flavour your life and the game of cricket actually lets you explore those because you can be out there dreaming. You can't be concentrating intently all the time. It's unique to our sport. People often ask what is said in the middle. Those little team meetings are often a distraction. It could be commentary on someone in the crowd or a fight you have just seen or another location you'd love to be at at that moment. Alfie [Justin Langer] would always say, 'You wouldn't be dead for quids.' That was his big catch cry in the middle as he stepped in to another bouncer and got smashed on the head. I guess what I'm saying is that it can't be all consuming.

I think if you're like that in anything in life you've lost the balance. I take time, I think, to try and understand what I'm feeling. I love paying attention to detail, to moments in life. In a wave you only get one chance to be in the right position on it or you're out of the wave.

In fishing there are only key bite phases, moon phases, tide phases that you can be in the game otherwise you might as well be cracking the tinnies or talking lies to your mates. But remain in the moment, that's where you need to be. I think the ocean, like a lot of my passions, gets me to a very inner space and cricket was exactly like that. Cricket was about my little office and someone else's little office.

And those offices come together and you shared that space and I could reveal who I was. It was a space which elevated my mindset to a gladiatorial position. Rank and position were important to my life, structures were important to my life and all of these passions. They are complete passions and they keep me so in the moment.

Playing with joy and freedom

ADAM GILCHRIST: I was an aggressive cricketer. Well, I don't know of many non-aggressive Australian cricketers! It was the culture we grew up in. I used to pester Dad to throw me countless balls, tennis balls, golf balls, cricket balls—whatever it may be. We'd do all this sort of technique work although I don't know that I ever had the greatest textbook technique. But at the end of it he would just throw me the ball just say 'Hit the ball, just whack it, just feel the ball in the middle and have fun.' So I think that was maintained as a basic philosophy. It sounds romantic, beautiful and great but doesn't sound so good when you're walking off the field first ball of the game when you've gone out to hit the ball and got out. So it's a tough one to stay true to. But, as a general rule, to me 'Hit the ball' means to have fun, to play with a bit of joy and freedom. Do everything as hard as you can and as well as you can and walk off and just be happy with what you've done.

I don't remember walking out to bat or sitting and waiting to bat and feeling under pressure because people expected me to walk out and blitz it, turn it on or play in a certain way. I never sat and thought about the quotes like 'Once in a generation' or 'One of the best ever'. That didn't weigh me down.

Probably towards the end of my career and post-2005 I hit some road bumps or hurdles. I was thinking I had achieved a level but was struggling to get to that standard. I was thinking was it a fluke—was I really good enough to get to that level? Did I just have a good run? Those little self-doubts were creeping in and they hadn't plagued me at all up to that time. That's where I had my greatest challenge—60 or 70 Test matches in to my career. A lot of guys come in on a rise then hit a slump and get dropped. That's when they have the doubts and question marks and they've got to rebuild.

And a lot of the best players do rebuild and come back in. But for me I had that difficult hurdle over three-quarters of the way through my career.

Never satisfied

ALLAN BORDER: I can honestly say I never walked off the ground 100 per cent satisfied. To me that was a driving force. Whether that's a good thing or a bad thing or a flaw or whatever it was just my make-up. So if you're never satisfied with a performance you know you're always driven to do better. I think that was my character. I was always driven because there was always a better performance in front of me. So that's a character trait. The longevity is luck. I had a few finger injuries and that type of thing but nothing that stopped me playing. If you are consistently free of injury you're going to have a long career.

At the end I was mentally exhausted and you start to realise that your game is not at the level that it once was. You know you do lose that fraction with age. Father Time catches up with everyone. If I'm brutally honest I probably played at least 12 months longer than I should have. But there was the carrot of playing against South Africa in a Test series. If I had my time over again I probably should have retired after England in 1993. I could feel my game starting to go, you know, falling below a standard that I felt comfortable with.

I was starting to take short cuts and mentally you just start to get a bit exhausted with the process of keeping yourself at that level of play and captaining the side. If I had my time over I probably should have retired a year earlier.

In the zone

SHANE WARNE: To play and perform at your best as an individual is about being prepared, about happiness and feeling fresh. You've got to have a clear mind. Do whatever you have to do—ring your friends, ring your missus, sort out some business stuff, sponsorship, calendar, schedules. People then talk about being 'in the zone'.

Being 'in the zone' is being able to concentrate on what you are doing right now with no distractions. When someone talks or refers to the 'zone' it's 100 per cent concentration on what they're doing at that very moment. That's preparation. That's what I think. I could be completely wrong but it worked for me.

As far as playing the game goes I never saw it as a job. And I don't like cricketers or sportsmen saying: It's my job to score goals for Chelsea; it's my job to bowl as fast as I can to take wickets for Australia; it's my job to kick goals for the St Kilda footy club. I don't think sport should be a job. I do understand that sport now is big business. I understand whether it be TV rights or big player contracts there are responsibilities you have with getting paid big dollars. I understand all that but I think my mindset and outlook was always about this as my hobby. This is my passion and I love it. I love the game and I'll do anything to be the best I possibly can and for my country and whoever I'm playing with, whether it's St Kilda Cricket Club, Victoria, Hampshire, the Royals, Australia. I had exactly the same mindset and it was fun.

Too many sports these days are all about PR, brand and all that sort of stuff and sometimes because it's the responsibility to the public to be seen to be doing the right thing, you've got to say the right thing. You can't be controversial. I think we're losing characters in sport. It's an entertainment. People want to see sport and people want to see movies. So if you can make them as entertaining as you possibly can with a bit of colour, with a bit of flair, with a bit of fun, with a smile on your face no matter what, where there's a bit of drama. Then people will pay to watch and walk away and say: 'God, I loved the cricket today.' And that's important.

Too many players don't realise that there's a big bad world out there, there's a lot of other things happening. When you play for Australia you sort of live in a bubble and the only thing that's important is your own form and the next game and how you are going and you sort of lose track of the most important things.

Another message I have for any sportsman is to grow your friends. I was lucky that I had quite diverse friends outside of the game, a big variety of diverse friends. It wasn't just cricket. That wasn't my life and I think if that's all you do it's hard to get out of that rut. Have friends or acquaintances that you can have dinner with in different parts of the world. Go and have a look at a museum or in India get in a tuk-tuk and go and see the snake charmer across the road from the Taj. Do a few things which sort of make you feel pretty relaxed about the cricket.

The game should always be played to win and within the rules. There are certain things you don't do on the field but do whatever it takes to win. You've just got to win. Keep the sportsmanship, keep the camaraderie but you do everything you know within the rules because winning is a lot more enjoyable than just doing okay.

Uncomplicated

BILL LAWRY: I had no philosophy, I wasn't that complicated. My attitude was to win at all costs and not to lose at all costs. People didn't think this about me but I always wanted to win, everybody wants to win. But I hated losing more than . . . I loved winning, of course, but I think it's like a captain in a war on a ship. If you're getting a hiding you don't want the ship to sink and that's how I felt about being captain. I felt that you try and win but if you can't win you do anything you can to save the game. That's the way I captained the side but I'm not a cricket . . . probably unfortunately . . . I'm not a cricket vegetable [tragic]. I think probably my captaincy suffered a bit like that. I hated dressing-rooms. I only liked to be in a dressing-room when I got changed to go out to bat. I hated dressing-rooms after the game. I think a lot of the guys like Ian Chappell and others—they loved dressing-rooms. They'd talk cricket folklore and I wasn't into all that. I just loved the competition.

Inner toughness

MIKE ATHERTON: It was very important to me to lead from the front—set the right example both on and off the field. What I hoped to do, and probably failed to do, but hoped to do was to change the English team from being a fairly disparate bunch of cricketers who came from their counties and went back to their counties. I hoped to make the England team almost like a nineteenth county where we had a more stable structure and a stronger kind of team ethic and team culture. I don't think that happened naturally. It couldn't happen until central contracts came in a few years later. But that was the hope and the aim at that time to identify a group of young and talented players—the likes of [Nasser] Hussain, [Graham] Thorpe and [Mark] Ramprakash and myself and take England forward in a spirited kind of way.

I had an inner toughness or strength, if you like, some kind of confidence in what I was doing, in the method, but I never thought of myself as a hard nut. I mean, what is toughness? What is hardness? It comes in many shapes and forms. I mean if you put me in a boxing ring with somebody I'd be hopeless. I've never thrown a punch in my life. But that's not toughness and I wouldn't put myself in that field. If you play over a period of time and you do reasonably well then you realise you can mix it with some of the best players around and that instils some kind of confidence. So if I did have toughness, it just came from confidence in what I was doing and I never perceived myself as a hard nut at all.

When I started to play first-class cricket and was on the verge of playing for England, Australia were obviously just resurgent under Allan Border. They played a particular style and type of cricket so I wasn't surprised when I came in in 1989 and to the brand of cricket they were playing. There were no referees. It's so different now. I mean Merv Hughes, for example, bless his soul, would give you a gob-full after every ball and that's how it was. You played in that era that's how things were. It wasn't surprising to me. I made a very early conscious decision to try and get to know these blokes because it kind of humanised them in a way. I wasn't one to go into the Australian dressing-room for a beer at the end of every day's play. That wasn't how it happened but at the end of the game I tried to get to know someone like Merv Hughes because then you realise that he's probably like everyone else. How did I react to it as a batsman? I didn't try to get engaged in a verbal contest with the bowler. Ultimately no one wins that, I think, so a wry smile and stare and let him turn around. You have to have faith in your players and trust that they are going to play the game in the right way. And most people did. I think sledging sometimes is overdone, particularly once the match referees came in in 1993 and climbed on to behaviour. To my mind Test cricket players behave pretty well and going back to playing league in the north of England was a much more terrifying experience in some ways. Most English Test players that I played with played the game in the right way. You have to recognise it's a red-blooded game and you get caught up in the moment occasionally but you have to give them a bit of latitude if you can.

THE FOUNDATION STONE
OF
NIVEDITA BHAVAN
(UDAYAN GIRLS WING)
WAS LAID BY
STEVE WAUGH
AUSTRALIAN CRICKET CAPTAIN
AND
PATRON, UDAYAN
ON
JULY 21ST

A growing number of elite cricketers have become aligned with charitable foundations and causes as the money circulating within the game has increased exponentially. Successful Australian captain Steve Waugh is renowned for his philanthropic work in Australia and India. One of his finest achievements was the establishment of a dormitory for girls at Udayan, a rehabilitation home for the children of leprosy sufferers at Barrackpore on the outskirts of Kolkata.

In 1963 Australian prime minister Bob Menzies was knighted and Sir Donald Bradman emerged from retirement for his leader's match against Ted Dexter's touring Englishmen. To the disappointment of the crowd, Bradman survived only five deliveries before playing on to his wicket by way of his foot. Dexter (far right) co-authored 'The Preamble—The Spirit of Cricket' which proclaims the Laws of Cricket. This triumvirate placed great store in the traditional values and virtues of the game.

CHAPTER SIX

The spirit of cricket

For more than 200 years the symbolic spirit of the game was implicitly understood by cricketers. It was a divine covenant that needed not to be spoken or written.

The ink was still drying on the formal proclamation of the colony of New South Wales when the first formal code of laws of cricket was adopted by the Marylebone Cricket Club (MCC) on 30 May 1788.

So profound was the change to the mood and mores of societies in the post-colonial cricket world that by the time Australia celebrated its bicentenary in 1988, cricket's governors spoke of the need to be explicit rather than implicit to ensure the preservation of the game's traditional values.

The decade from 1977 was arguably the most tumultuous since formalised Test matches began in 1877 and the game's elite players increasingly marched to the beat of different drums. It was a period punctuated by player dissatisfaction and rebellion and the stunning disempowerment of the game's crusty and intransigent establishment.

Sniffing the winds of change, the MCC chose the dawning of the new millennium as the appropriate time for the first major revision of the laws since the 1980 Code had updated and refined the versions of 1884 and 1947.

As the MCC Laws of Cricket Rewrite Working Party went about its business, former England captains Colin Cowdrey and Ted Dexter turned their attention to what was commonly viewed as a worrisome deterioration in player behaviour from the international arena to club and school grounds.

Lord Cowdrey, a former president of the MCC and one of England's greatest and most loved sporting identities, was renowned for his unwavering belief in and warm embrace of the game's lofty principles and rich traditions.

Dexter, himself a Lord, at least in the minds of his countless admirers and newspaper and magazine headline writers, succeeded Cowdrey as chairman of the pivotal MCC cricket sub-committee in 1999 and was as anxious as his predecessor about the falling of behavioural standards in the game.

England's most attacking and thrilling batsman of the 1960s and an adventurer by nature, Dexter was also a very accomplished golfer who impressed professionals with the power and majesty of his game.

And after considerable thought it was to this ancient individual pursuit that he turned in an attempt to eradicate the ills which had beset cricket.

In June 2011, 12 years after he first workshopped his idea with Cowdrey, Dexter explained the genesis of 'The Spirit of Cricket' which so conspicuously became the Preamble to the revised laws of the game on 3 May 2000—just seven months before the death of Cowdrey at the age of 67.

Appropriately he gave his interview for this archive in the sumptuous clubrooms of the internationally renowned Sunningdale Golf Club in Berkshire during a sojourn to England from his home in Nice, France.

At 76 and frustrated that a chronic back complaint limited his time on the course during his visit, Dexter had clear recall of the 'reports of awful behaviour in schools cricket' that constantly came across the desk of MCC secretary Roger Knight in the 1990s. At the same time, nearby in his modest office adjacent to the Father Time stand, the International Cricket Council's first chief executive, Australian David Richards, was confronted with similar complaints about declining standards of behaviour on the international stage.

Subduing if not utterly disillusioning for the true believers reared in a simpler age, the time had come to formally define the ethereal spirit of cricket.

'I talked to Colin Cowdrey about the etiquette of golf,' said Dexter, who captained England in 30 Test matches between 1961 and 1964.

'I said golf has rules and etiquette is rule number one. The only place that "spirit of cricket" appeared in our laws was under

"Fair and unfair play" which said the captain shall be responsible not only for the conduct of the game, not only within the laws but within the spirit of the game.

'This was the only time those words were mentioned in the whole of the laws. So we said why don't we sort of lift that out and just spell out what we think we mean by it.'

And so, 'The Preamble—The Spirit of Cricket', was written.

> *Cricket is a game that owes much of its unique appeal to the fact that it should be played not only within its Laws but also within the Spirit of the Game. Any action which is seen to abuse this spirit causes injury to the game itself. The major responsibility for ensuring the spirit of fair play rests with the captains.*

Reference is also made under Law 42 Fair and unfair play.

1. Fair and unfair play—responsibility of captains
   The responsibility lies with the captains for ensuring the play is conducted with the spirit and traditions of the game as described in The Preamble—The Spirit of Cricket, as well as within the laws.

'The other interesting thing was when it came to the moment when we got it all,' said Dexter.

'Lord Griffiths was sort of in the chair and we asked whether we can embody this in the laws.

'He said: "Ah, we would have to have an AGM with all the MCC members if we were to put in the laws. It should be a preamble to the laws. Shall we carry on." And that is what it is now.

'You know, it thrilled me the other day to hear Michael Atherton, who is a marvellous commentator on the game, cerebral, good thinker etcetera, saying how the conduct of players on the field at international level had improved out of all knowledge.

'I like to think that our work on the spirit of the game was effective and the MCC has supported it very well. I mean it's cost them plenty of money every year but they have a good budget to support the Spirit of Cricket and I think it seems to have worked.'

It was evident conducting the interviews for the Bradman International Cricket Hall of Fame archive that while the intent of 'The Spirit of Cricket' preamble is patently clear its fundamental worth is interpreted in various ways.

While many traditionalists were affronted that the meaning of the spirit of cricket needed to be spelled out, no longer could it be presumed that such an ethos was an intrinsic aspect of the game.

Respect for the game and its moral code had to be legislated. The new millennium was a different time.

> **HENRY OLONGA**: To me it's all about commonsense respect for the opposition, really. I mean, you care about this great spirit the game has because we're different from football, aren't we? It's not the same as a ruffians' game. I was going to say rugby, but rugby's not bad, actually. They respect the referee, at least. To me you're sending the wrong message to kids if you're an international sportsman and you're seen showing dissent, arguing with umpires, fighting, showing violence, swearing loudly near a mike. The antithesis of that is that

we have sportsmen, cricketers, who are well behaved, who clap when a batsman's done well, appreciate good cricket, play within the confines of the rules of the game not just the spirit of the game. To me the spirit of cricket is all about maintaining the highest levels of integrity and morality by being an honest cricketer.

WES HALL: I came up at a time when the three Ws [Worrell, Weekes, Walcott] were, you know, the most dominant batsmen in the most triumphant team in the world. When you come up under that type of excellence you see what they put back into the game. The spirit of the game was fantastic then. The West Indies were the only multi-racial side in the world and it was really a rainbow coalition in a world that was not particularly good at ethnic diversity. So, I mean having the three Ws, Ramadhin and Valentine, those senior men, there was no sledging. Sir Frank [Worrell] made sure we didn't portray that happy-go-lucky syndrome any more. We wanted the spectators to receive all types of play with approbation.

We wanted not only to make friends and influence people but we wanted to prove that West Indians are not just the calypso cricketers mooted for so long. We wanted to be able to win in good places against good sides, England and Australia. We wanted to do that. Having done that I thought our job would be to pass the baton on—you know, make sure that the youngsters who were coming on would one day fit perfectly into the pantheon of those great players that had passed. That's the spirit of the game the way I know it. You see, we played for very little so the spirit of the game was loving the game; what it meant to us and to our country and our total development in the Caribbean. That was important to us.

ANIL KUMBLE: It means not just how you play the game but how you can uphold the qualities of the game and the rules of the game. Yes, you need to be aggressive and you need to be winning at all times. There are times when things go out of control but when those situations happen I think you need to be aware of the game itself. If you have the larger interests of the game in mind at all times then the spirit of the game takes care of itself. It is when the individual gets bigger than the game—that's when the spirit gets affected in my opinion. If you know you're just one of those millions of people who've played this game and loved the game and play it for the love of the game then the spirit automatically takes care of itself. I think that's something which we need to instil in all young cricketers.

RAHUL DRAVID: Don Bradman said that this is a great game and in the short time that we have we have a responsibility to carry the game forward and to make it a better game than when we started. And I think that is really what the spirit means. Playing the game hard, playing it fair and enjoying whatever comes with it. You know, learning to deal with the success, learning to deal with the failure and learning to be about whatever you achieve and being graceful whenever you don't succeed.

BISHAN BEDI: What does the spirit of the game mean to me? Everything, everything you know. You don't challenge an umpire's decision and you don't sledge. There are many 'don'ts', you know. If you feel you're out, you walk. Okay. Don't leave it to the judgement of the umpire, go by conscience. And if the catch hasn't been taken don't appeal for it. Don't appeal for LBW when you know the ball is clearly going down the leg side. Don't pressurise umpires. Umpires are as human as you are. And another thing that comes readily to mind. Don't chuck. That's not cricket. Why do we say 'It's not cricket.' It's an English proverb, you know. We never say 'It's not football, or it's not hockey, or it's not tennis, or it's not golf.' No, it is always associated with cricket because cricket is associated directly with uprightness, and honesty and integrity.

DANIEL VETTORI: I do believe the spirit is the reason a lot of us play. The nature of the game lends itself to so many different situations, happenings—making quick judgements and trying to make right judgements all the time. I think all cricketers have been involved on the right side of it and the wrong side of it. But ultimately, when you finish and have a beer at the end of the day, we want to sit there on the right side of it because this is important to everyone. You want to play hard but to think that all those people out there watch you and admire you because you played within the spirit of the game. I think it is something every player would love to have as a legacy when they leave the game.

FRANK TYSON: The spirit of the game means to me playing cricket to enjoy the process of playing cricket; playing cricket to win a game of cricket, playing cricket by means that satisfy you in terms of moral behaviour and that means on the field and off the field. I don't see any enjoyment whatsoever, any satisfaction whatsoever in going out into the middle of a cricket ground and playing cricket and winning a game if you have not done it in a way that your mother and father would have liked.

And I mean that seriously. My parents were very moral in respect that they expected hard work would be rewarded and they expected you to observe that ethic. I think that's a great sort of criterion you've got to observe. Do it but do it well and do it fairly. This is why I have great objections to people who indulge in sledging or anything that denotes sharp practice. What's the point in breaking a record if you come off the ground knowing that you'd done your bit but done it in a completely amoral way.

BARRY RICHARDS: Times have changed. You know, in the early days, 'walking' was just an accepted part of it. That started to evolve when the umpires got more technology and they call shots in terms of making the decision. But I'd like to think that the spirit of the game is still alive and well. One of the things that disappoints me, I guess, is that there's so much emphasis on the player. You know, the warm down, the ice bath, the getting back to the hotel, the things in their ears. There's no interaction between the two teams and I find that very disappointing. I don't say you've got to live in each other's pockets but it would be nice if you have interaction—particularly teams from different cultures being able to share a beer or even a soft drink. Just spend a bit of time with each other. But it seems everybody wants to keep everybody apart and the players insulated from the real world. I think that's a little disappointing for the spirit of cricket because I think the spirit of cricket is all-encompassing with a lot of countries and if you keep separating the people for whatever reason you lose that little bit of the spirit of cricket.

ANDREW STRAUSS: You know I think we're very fortunate in the game of cricket that we have this link with tradition. I suppose cricket sort of stands out as a bit of a beacon in terms of the fact that there's more to sport than just winning. For me the spirit is about being respectful to the rules of the game, being respectful to the umpires, the officials. Play hard, definitely, but within boundaries.

I'm pleased where we are as a game at the moment. I think a lot of other sports have drifted off and got more and more competitive but at the same time respect for officials and other players has drifted off as well. I don't think that's happened in cricket as much as in other sports.

JONATHAN AGNEW: The spirit of cricket means respecting your opponent first and foremost, playing the game hard but fair, being honest. I think that's essentially it and to be able to have a drink with your opponents in the bar afterwards. It's about integrity. I can get a bit stroppy sometimes when I see somebody, in my opinion, pushing it to the limit. Captains sometimes do it, players sometimes do it and that does make me cross because I think most people try and play within that spirit. Really, when you look back through history the current players have the game in their hands for a twinkling of an eye. It's theirs for a fleeting moment and I do get a bit crotchety when I see somebody treating the game with disrespect because it's the next generation of people who will see that and I don't want them to copy it. Things like the DRS [Decision Review System], which I don't like. I worry about the next generation—or they're in the club grounds and schools now—who are going to be objecting to an umpire's decision. They haven't got DRS but it doesn't matter and they will say to an umpire 'I saw Kevin Pietersen doing that on the telly and I think you're wrong.'

You have to respect the umpire and you've got to take the rough with the smooth in cricket. It's what makes you as a character, I think. You have to accept that not everything is fair in this world. If you're a batsman and you've been sawn off, well, tough, because actually tomorrow you might get away with one. Taking it on the chin, I think, makes cricket such an important educating school for kids. They have to learn that not all is going to go well in life.

MIKE BREARLEY: You play as hard as you can but within a framework of respect for the other players, the umpires and spectators, but especially the other players and umpires. And humour, I hope, comes into it from time to time even in the fiercest matches. The opposition have been through a match in the same way and you rely on them for testing your skills and playing the game properly. There is a fellow feeling with the opposition, especially at the end of a Test match. You may not be aware of it during it but at the end of it or the end of a series when you sit down and realise that these people are ordinary human beings with their own vulnerabilities and own strengths. You know, that sort of mutual respect comes through and that's very enjoyable.

JOHN WRIGHT: The spirit means respecting the laws of the game and respecting the people you play with and against so that you can always walk off the park, go to the mirror, look at yourself in it and be quite happy with the person you're looking at.

RICHARD HADLEE: There are values and there's a lot of history to learn about. I remember one particular game that Dad [Walter Hadlee] played, in fact he was captain, when the English came out to New Zealand. In simple terms, Cyril Washbrook was given out LBW [the First Test at Lancaster Park, Christchurch in March 1951] and Dad said to him as he walked back to the pavilion: 'You hit that, Cyril, didn't you?' Cyril said: 'Yes, I did,' and Dad said: 'Wait there a minute.' He went to the umpire and said they wished to withdraw the appeal and recall the batsman, which was duly done.

I think Cyril went on to score 50 odd [58] but in Dad's mind he did the right thing and therefore the team conscience was clear. Well, there is tremendous value and spirit of the game in that. Sometimes when you are so competitive and get frustrated you can lose a little about what the game is about.

DAVID GOWER: Spirit means all sorts of things. I think it's a game you want to play fairly at all times if you possibly can. I think you acknowledge as a player at international level that there are weak moments where there is the . . . what is it . . . I don't know . . . the sense of patriotism, the sense of loyalty to your team, the sense of pig-headedness, a sense of selfishness. Whatever it might be, you have to admit you edge one and you don't walk. You think maybe that was wrong but you defend yourself as best you can because there are very few in this game now who'll look back on their careers and say, 'I never got it wrong, never got it wrong.'

There are always things that you can look back on which I think are a gentle stain on the game. I think at the same time you come to terms with those things you need to be able to play the game in the spirit that says: I am going to compete as hard as I physically can and mentally can; I am going to respect my opponent for everything that he is; I'm going to try and win, not necessarily at all costs, but I'm going to do everything I can to win and to succeed and to play a part in that victory for my team.

I think on a good day all that clicks into place and on a bad day your own disappointments sometimes cloud the day.

Sure, your own personal failings will cloud a day but then you have the team spirit, which is a very hard thing to define. And then you have, you know, the spirit of the game—the whole ethos of the game. Team spirit is the thing that keeps you together at any one time—10 other blokes who are part of your team who are there with you to support you. It's vitally important to have good friends through a career. I think this is something that keeps you going because there's always going to be times when you're not at your best and you just need someone to bounce off, someone to get you up again, to build you up again. That's vital, desperately important within your own team.

But at the same time I always found it enjoyable and more than worthwhile to get to know the enemy. I always found it interesting to know more about the opposition, whether it be in Australia, the West Indies, wherever. In Australia it was always much easier because of the tradition that you go and have a beer at the end of the day. You sit in the rooms, no rush.

When we finish the beers we'll go. That's how I got to know a couple of Chappells, a Lillee, a Thomson, a Marsh, a Border, a Merv Hughes a Rodney Hogg—you know these people who might have been trying to knock your head off for the previous six or seven hours. They became proper people and I thought that was vitally important. I thought that was, you know, very much part of the spirit of my game because at the end of each day I didn't hold any grudges against people. If we'd lost, so be it—the opposition probably played better. If we'd won then I was proud that we'd played better. And if I'd done something worthy myself then I was proud of that too.

I look back on those 18 years or so of professional cricket knowing I got on with a lot of people; knowing I'd made a lot of friends. Sadly you can disappear once you've finished playing, once you lose contact. You know they just drift into the background again. But at the time and in order to enjoy the game to its fullest you need to appreciate the game and you need to appreciate the people who play it.

KAPIL DEV: I think you have to be honest. I always enjoyed the spirit of the game the way the West Indies played in the 1970s and 1980s. They never used to talk too much. In recent times there's too much talk and too much abusive language going on. You don't need that. When ability and talent is there you can perform better than other people. The bat and ball should talk. In the last 15 years things have changed from bad to worse even though the ICC has done a great job to make some rules, which is good. You have to have discipline but you can't have the same cricket we had 50 years back. A gentleman's game it's not and we should not even expect that. A lot of careers and lives depend on a lot of people so it's very tough. One bad decision from the umpire can finish somebody's life.

GRAEME POLLOCK: There's an amazing spirit and I think it's a fantastic game. We were isolated for 22 years but I did play in quite a few Rest of the World sides with West Indian,

Indian and Pakistani cricketers. And they were fantastic people. I think the spirit is you get treated as a cricketer, that's the yardstick. I'm not a politician. We came out of apartheid in the 1960s and I remember playing for the first Rest of the World team in 1966 [in the obscure Rothman World Cup and, in a sense, a forerunner to the inaugural World Cup in 1975]. We didn't know what to expect. There was Colin Bland, myself, Eddie Barlow and my brother Peter and we had Wes Hall and Charlie Griffith, Garry Sobers and Lance Gibbs. That first meeting was something we didn't really look forward to because, you know, I mean the reputation of South Africans and white South Africans wasn't great at all. But I think that we were seen as cricketers and judged as cricketers. I think that is where the spirit eliminates all those extra things where you're seen as racist or you're this or you're that.

MATTHEW HAYDEN: The spirit of cricket means you hold true to your core values. Australia will never win a Spirit of Cricket Award because competition is confused with aggressive behaviour and egotistical awareness and it's absolute rubbish. I mean, we're not out in the middle to play tiddlywinks. We are Australia and from dust we built and from dust we'll remain. But we'll remain there together as mates. I think there's a great spirit of Australia and I'm proud of that. I'm proud of the fact that I was part of that—that I felt a part of the Anzac. I mean when you go to places like Gallipoli you feel the spirit of great Australians that have gone before you in battle. When you go to Villers-Bretonneux and the

Battle of the Somme, there's this beautiful sign, 'Never forget Australians.' We have a great fighting culture, a great spirit and one that I will defend, or have defended, with honour and passion 'til I die.

GLENN McGRATH: The spirit of the game means a lot of different things to different people and also to different cultures. I think the Australian way is having respect for the game and playing good hard aggressive cricket but within the boundaries and not becoming personal. You never want to let your teammates down out in the middle and it's about being true to yourself and giving everything you've got and then walking off the field at the end of the day, win, lose or draw, knowing you've backed yourself. You know you gave everything and played within the rules so it's a combination of things. I think it means a lot of different things to different people but that's what it means to me.

BOB SIMPSON: Tough competitive cricket played with respect for the opposition. I think that sums it up pretty well. I'm appalled at the amount of sledging that goes on today and sledging which is verbal even to the public. They can hear it all and to me it's often frustration. But it also shows a lack of confidence in talent to have to resort to some means to get a person out.

SIMON TAUFEL: To me the spirit means an absolute level of fairness and consideration and respect for your opponent without considering the result. By that I mean there is a classic moment in the Edgbaston Test in 2005 where Australia had tried really hard to get over the line. They fell a few runs short with England bowling them out and I remember an image of the really dejected Brett Lee down on his haunches and Andrew Flintoff coming to him and putting his hand on his shoulder to console him. At a moment when Andrew should have been celebrating victory and all that had been achieved in the match his priority was consoling his opponent. He was showing a level of fairness and consideration and respect for his opponent above celebrating the victory and to me that's what the spirit of cricket is all about. It's the way that you play the game. It's the way you want to be remembered for the way you play the game and not necessarily just your results. That's the spirit of cricket to me—that fairness and consideration and respect for your opponent over and above the result of the match and personal milestones or achievements.

RICHIE BENAUD: Colin Cowdrey and Ted Dexter put together 'The Spirit of Cricket' that is now the preamble to the laws of cricket. Before that happened I don't know whether you 'did' the spirit of cricket. But my brother [John] and I were 'doing' the spirit of cricket because of our father at breakfast, lunch and dinner when we always talked about cricket. The spirit of cricket came into it there but not in the same way as it [does] now. Father taught us how to behave whether we did well or badly, won or lost, if things were going well on the field or not. And he instilled in us a love of the game but also the spirit of cricket.

MARK TAYLOR: The spirit of cricket to me means always remembering it's just a game—something that Rick McCosker said to me at the Newcastle Sports Ground in my third year as a state cricketer. I wasn't playing very well and he said to me after I'd missed out: 'Mark, remember, it's just a game.' I sort of snapped back at him and he said 'The more that you can keep it as just a game the more you'll enjoy it and the better the game will be.' I think that's a great summary of how you should play cricket. As the years have gone by in my time the game has become more, well, not professional, but people get paid more money for playing it. I think the people who play it the best are the guys who remember it's just a game. People don't die. Well, people generally don't die from games of cricket and I think if you can keep that in the back of your mind when you play or lead a side then you'll be a much better cricketer.

IAN CHAPPELL: To me the spirit of cricket is a load of bollocks. You just play to the laws. The laws of the game are there and if you play to the laws of the game then you are playing to the spirit of the game. Let the umpires control the game. I've had discussions with people over balls being called on the first bounce and so on. I say, look, it's a simple question. You've got to ask yourself—would I like to be cheated out of my wicket? Unless you're an absolute dope or a liar the answer to that is 'No'. Then why would you do it to someone else? You know, to me, it's pretty simple. I was brought up to play hard but fair. They were the words my father Martin always said. One of the greatest tributes I've seen was from Clive Lloyd who wrote in his book: 'I have played a lot of cricket against the Chappell brothers—it's always been hard but fair.' I thought to myself if Martin read that he'd be happy because that's the way he brought us up.

ALAN DAVIDSON: Well I think our spirit of cricket is totally different to the one that's written today. The one that's written today is written by the players. I believe the heritage and history of the game and the game we were brought up with. The opportunity I had when I worked in town. We had three sports stores in town run by Bert Oldfield, Stan McCabe and Alan Kippax, and I spent lunch times with them and they talked about the games they played in and the spirit in which it was played.

Today you see appeals going up for everything and anything. You'd never appeal much. Sometimes you'd go up for an appeal and you'd realise the bloke got a nick into the inside pad and as soon as you'd appealed you'd say, 'Sorry, ump.' It was a natural remark that came from you. Today you get blokes ranting on and carrying on trying to influence the umpire to make a decision, which is not what I call the spirit of the game.

I think these are the things where it is different. You've got to have some sort of discipline. You have to respect the game you play more than anything else. I think Sir Donald Bradman once said the game has got to be better for you being in it. And I think it's a pretty important part of what I call the spirit of cricket, the spirit of the game. The game was always looked upon if something untoward happened—even in non-cricketing areas. It isn't cricket. I think no better terminology could be given.

MIKE HUSSEY: It is very important that the game is played in the right manner. It is not difficult to play in the right manner but you have to play as hard as you possibly can and you have to play to win but you have to play the game fairly as well and play within the rules. I know the Australian team is sometimes criticised because of how hard we play the game but I can honestly say we do play within the rules and play fairly all the time. I think it is really important that we realise that we are custodians of the game and it is important to set an example to future Australian teams and, probably future teams around the world. The game is more important than any one individual and any one result. We must keep the game in good hands going forward.

ALLAN BORDER: It's sometimes hard to define. Playing in the right spirit is an old cricketing term, isn't it! From an Australian point of view we like to think we play a hard, uncompromising game but in the right way. So we're within the laws. I always find it hard to define what the spirit of the game might mean. It's just the way the game is meant to be played. We maybe have a harder edge than others the way we play it. Maybe it's our convict blood. I don't know. It's just the way we play and I always feel we play it in what I would call the right spirit.

ADAM GILCHRIST: For me the key ingredient of the spirit of cricket is respect: the word 'respect'. So respecting your opponent, your umpire and your administrator, which it seems has been a testing relationship throughout cricket history. But it's respect for yourself, too. So I think without that there's no spirit of cricket. There's no use talking about the spirit of cricket unless that's there as the main ingredient. No doubt there are testing times when you look back and say: Did I show total and utter respect? Only you can make that decision and only you can learn from whatever the answer is at that time.

CLIVE LLOYD: It is important. I'm sorry we didn't have it before and we wouldn't have had that little blip in New Zealand [in 1979–80]. Sometimes you get caught up in trying to do well. At the same time you want to have the best people engaged in running the match. I think if we had had the technology and referees none of these things would have happened. I think the game is now seen in a different light. Unfortunately we have had a match-fixing situation. As far as I'm concerned cricket is about honesty and integrity and fair play. That stands out. You know, you always say 'It's not cricket.' You never say 'It's not football' or 'It's not hockey'.

BRIAN LARA: The spirit means everything. I believe that the 22 players should exactly understand the game, its legacy and how it can build character. What it stands for. You see a lot of youngsters coming up and moving from arrogance to being proper human beings and captains of their countries and ambassadors. I believe the spirit of the game is something we should cherish, something we should always push to the forefront. The spirit of the game is something everyone should wear on their sleeve.

BILL LAWRY: I don't think you need that, really. I think it gets back to your upbringing, coming through the grades. Maybe the problem today is that most Test and Shield players and the Twenty20 players don't come through the ranks playing against Test players, talking to them and seeing their demeanour. I was in awe when I played against Richmond as Bill Johnston and Doug Ring were in the side and they came and spoke to you after the game.

I think today young guys are thrown in and it's a different marketplace. The spirit of the game is really down to strength of umpires and the captains. But you don't want to take the flair out of the game either. I think there's a fine line between flair and stepping over the line and I think that's where we've probably got to be careful. I think 99 per cent of the players of my era understood the spirit of the game because we were brought up to respect every level of cricket. Most of these guys today probably hardly ever play a district game. They come in the Under-19s and they're recognised and they're thrown into some squad and it's a completely different marketplace. But I think professional sportsmen generally have got as much respect for the game as amateur people. I honestly believe that. But there is always going to be a controversy or two and that's just the marketplace.

GRAEME SMITH: The spirit of the game is a crucial aspect. I mean, I definitely love the game being most competitive. I really do. It's an international sport and you know the challenge of playing another quality country and facing an incredible bowler from another team is really something. The competitive nature of sport is something I really enjoy. As time goes on I think you realise your role in society, your role as a sportsman and how kids really look up to you. So I think the spirit of the game is crucial and I know the International Cricket Council is very big on it.

As captain you have a massive role to play in all of those things so it's something I've sort of grown into in the captaincy and understood more than when I was young. I think little things like walking out in Sydney with a broken hand [January 2009] you realise that you affect people's lives more than by just the runs you score or the wickets you take and the games you win. You have a massive influence on people, so there have been a lot of different perspectives for me, which has been good.

JOEL GARNER: I would not change anything that I did in my years of playing cricket. The only thing I would do differently is that I would start five years earlier. I think if you played cricket at the top for 10 years and you didn't have friends from the teams that you played against or from travelling and visiting places you'd have wasted 10 years of your life. To me walking into dressing-rooms at the end of the game was the biggest part of it no mind that we were combatants in the middle. Everything that happened in the middle of the field happened and that was it. There's nothing wrong with me coming into your dressing-room and drinking a beer or two and we're all talking. Some of my best friendships are from on the cricket field. Rodney Hogg and I are the greatest of friends, not only from being opponents but from the time we spend. Greg Chappell, Thommo [Jeff Thomson], [Dennis] Lillee and Marshie [Rod Marsh]: Those were the fellows who came into the room with a six-pack any day irrespective of what happened. Some of the players didn't drink but they still walked into the room, walked in with their soft drinks and they sat down and talked. I think that is the greatest part of playing sport—talking to other people, meeting other people, making friends. Mudassar Nazar from Pakistan to me is a great bloke and we are the best of friends. You go through every team and you see, know the people that you can relate to. This is the great thing about playing a sport.

Irrepressible tyro David Hookes gives Tony Greig his comeuppance with this bold pull shot for three runs in the 46th over of Australia's second innings of the Centenary Test at the MCG in March 1977. Robustly sledged by Greig in Australia's first innings, Hookes took his revenge on the England captain by famously smiting him for five consecutive boundaries in the 57th over. Doug Walters and umpire Tom Brooks follow the trajectory of the ball.

CHAPTER SEVEN

Humour and hubris

The little man in the grey cardigan

There is the faux pas and there is the irredeemable social catastrophe.

In the spring of 1971 as the isolation of the iniquitous Old South Africa intensified, the two greatest cricketers of the 20th century pooled their intellects and resources to ensure a World XI replaced the blackballed Springbok team in Australia for the 1971–72 season.

Nearing the end of his second term as chairman of the then Australian Board of Control for International Cricket, Sir Donald Bradman implored his friend Garry Sobers to lead the World XI and enliven the summer with robust international competition and so prepare the Australian team for the challenge of an Ashes series in 1972.

Sobers, who was destined to be knighted in 1975, had carried all before him the previous year leading a World XI to a 4–1 series win against England after the abandonment of South Africa's scheduled visit to the United Kingdom. He had scored 588 runs at 73.50 with two centuries and also was the most successful bowler with 21 wickets at 21.52.

After some hesitancy Sobers, 35 and close to retirement, was swayed by Bradman's persuasiveness. Certainly he was grateful to be honestly told the status of the matches Bradman planned as he was annoyed the Marylebone Cricket Club had reneged on its promise to add the Rest of the World matches to each player's Test match statistics.

In awe of Sobers and his accomplishments was the tall, blond 23-year-old South African-born Sussex all-rounder Tony Greig who was called up for the second 'Test' at Nottingham. Initially he was under the impression he was making his Test debut for England.

Sixteen months later Greig still was without a Test cap but had become so familiar to his idol that Sobers, with Bradman's imprimatur, chose him for the World XI for the Australian tour.

> **TONY GREIG**: My father, who was a real traditionalist, put me on the plane and I'll never forget his last words: 'Now look. You're going to meet the great man Bradman. Please do yourself a favour—listen and don't do too much talking. You may learn something.' My old man always thought that I spoke a little bit too much and didn't do enough listening. So that was the message as I was put on the plane. In Johannesburg

I met up with Hylton Ackerman [whose only international cricket was with the World XI] and off we went. In those days we had to land first in Perth and clear customs. As we came out there were four old guys who declared they were from the local Cricket Lovers' Society. They said they'd heard we were on the plane and had come out for a bit of a chat about cricket. So we went down to the coffee shop and talked cricket to these old blokes. Now, don't forget we are two youngsters wanting to have a look around and see what the young girls of Australia looked like. We were just so excited. So back on the plane we go and land at Adelaide. Now I didn't know that Bradman lived in Adelaide and I didn't know that Bradman would even consider coming to the airport in the early hours of the morning to meet Hylton Ackerman and Tony Greig. As it turned out there was this little man in a grey cardigan standing at the entrance of the old Adelaide Airport. My immediate reaction and that of Hylton's was that these Cricket Lovers' Society people were everywhere. We walked in and I didn't get his name. He made the same noises: 'Look, I thought I'd come out and meet you and have a bit of a chat about the tour. I've got a mate of mine, a guy called Ridings [former South Australian captain and prominent official Phil Ridings] ordering us a cup of coffee down the coffee shop.' So we gave him our holdalls as we had to get away from these guys. But we had to go to the coffee shop and we started talking about cricket. I don't think I did this because of the instructions from my father but I was listening a bit and this bloke seemed to be making quite a lot of sense. Eventually, in my moment of madness, I've actually turned to the great Sir Donald Bradman and looked him straight in the eye and I've said to him: 'Do you actually have anything to do with cricket around here?' Now, it was like water off a duck's back. Basically he said: 'Oh, the two of us run the local scene.' But for me it could have been the Airport Cricket Club for all I knew. So we just started talking again and the door flies open and in walks Garry Sobers.

I thought this is unbelievable, my captain has actually come to the airport to meet me. And of course here's my captain, my hero. I'm thinking he will come over to say good morning or hello to me so I stood up. And of course he's ignored me and gone straight to the great man and said 'Good morning, Sir Don.' Then I knew straight away the huge faux pas I'd made. We flew on to Melbourne and I talked to Hylton about it and decided we had to declare ourselves. So we told the story of what had happened and the Press phoned up Bradman. He said we were young boys and that there was no television in South Africa so how would we know him. He was very polite about it but the newspapers obviously wrote the story. By the time it got down to South Africa the headline was 'Greig snubs Bradman,' so that didn't impress my father too much. I met Bradman a lot and had quite a lot to do with him towards the end of his life. I remember one day knocking on his door at his home in Adelaide and he opened the door and, knowing I was coming, looked at me and said: 'You, do you have anything to do with cricket around here?' He just took the mickey out of me from then on and there was nothing I could do about that.

By Hookes or by crook

Five years after Sobers ensured the success of the World XI venture with a superlative innings of 254 that elicited high praise from Bradman, Greig returned to the Melbourne Cricket Ground for the Centenary Test as England's 58th captain.

It was, however, the 14th and last time that Greig held the office as word soon reached the game's crusty and crestfallen governors that he was in the vanguard of the World Series Cricket revolutionaries.

An unabashed extrovert loved and loathed in equal measure, Greig did not let his lofty position cruel his actions as an agent provocateur of the highest standing.

He has always dismissed as fanciful stories that he mocked and belittled 21-year-old David Hookes at a reception in advance of the Test so famously decided in Australia's favour by exactly the same 45-run margin as in the first Test match in March 1877.

He happily concedes, however, that words were spoken when Hookes, promoted after scoring five centuries in six innings of three consecutive Sheffield Shield matches for South Australia, came to the crease in Australia's first innings.

TONY GREIG: David Hookes was obviously a fantastic cricketer but I didn't know him from a bar of soap. He might have scored five centuries in the lead-up which is fantastic but I'd never heard of him. I was fielding at short leg when he came into bat. You know, this is one of those interesting aspects of the game I still wrestle with because I keep getting told it was Ian Chappell and his lot and my generation that introduced the next stage. That it used to be gentlemanly and when we came in it changed a bit because sledging, you know, became a little more pointed. It used to be nice and then it became nasty. Well, I think there is a bit of a point there. I think we started to get stuck into each other and this was an example. I was at silly point, I think, and bent down trying to put a bit of pressure on the young Hookes, this youngster who'd got this great reputation who was about to come in and smash us all around the ground. I said to him or to Knotty [wicketkeeper Alan Knott]: 'I wonder if his testicles have dropped,' or words to that effect. He backed off and said 'At least I'm playing for the country I was born in.' That's all that happened and that was in the first innings when he made a few runs [17]. It was the second innings where the memories will live forever and I will never be able to get away from them. When I brought myself on to bowl off-spinners there was a bit of rough outside the off stump to the left-hander and I thought if I could get it in there, I had a strong offside field, I could get one to just kick a little bit out of the rough. Because he played those big booming drives he might just hit one straight to cover. He hit one in the air between two fieldsmen and it could easily have gone either way. That was the first one, first or second one. But five in a row! The noise as each four went to the boundary . . . I'll never be allowed to forget that David Hookes hit me for five fours in a row at the MCG.

Metal v mettle

Greig's successor as England captain, Mike Brearley, opened the batting in the Centenary Test and quickly learned to withstand the taunts and jibes of Australian bowlers—and spectators—given to questioning his right to be in such exalted company.

It was as well he developed such a thick hide for 18 of his 31 Test matches in charge before being succeeded by Keith Fletcher were against Australia. And while individual success eluded him, England won 11 and lost four of these matches. And three of the four losses came in one three-match series in Australia in 1978–79 after the signing of the peace treaty with the World Series Cricket revolutionaries and the Ashes pointedly were not at stake.

Brearley was conscious that his undistinguished record as a Test batsman together with his bearing and an exceptional academic record at Cambridge University might inflame Australian crowds and even revive memories of his provocative Harlequin-capped predecessor Douglas Jardine in the infamous Bodyline series of 1932–33. He once explained: 'Temperamentally, I had to gird myself. The Australians are cocky but the British are more arrogant—that slightly superior thing which I know I have; clever with words, and if they rile me, I might become a bit snooty. That's exactly what would most annoy them.'

He led England to Australia in 1978–79 and again in 1979–80 and received as much advice on how to respond to vociferous Australian crowds as the techniques required to combat pace bowling generally and Rodney Hogg and Dennis Lillee in particular. Even Australian Council of Trade Unions (ACTU) president and future prime minister, Bob Hawke, a Rhodes Scholar to Oxford University in his sprightly cricket-playing days, warned him of the dangers of being perceived as a Jardinesque figure. But Brearley was not extroverted like Greig and found it difficult to interact with the outer crowds. As a consequence he was booed to the echo.

Lillee, who had dismissed Brearley in each innings of the Centenary Test, had quite a surprise in store for the England captain when they next met in a Test match at Perth just shy of three years later—the public presentation of the controversial, noisy, fabled aluminium bat. To the dismay of Brearley and his men, umpires Max O'Connell and Don Weser and the game's governors everywhere, Lillee chose a Test match with England to showcase his aluminium bat to an unsuspecting cricket community.

> **MIKE BREARLEY**: We knew it was going to happen or we'd heard it might be happening because there was a bit of pre-match publicity by Dennis. He came into bat just before the second new ball with the score about 7–250 [7–219] and the ball made a funny noise on the bat. We took the new ball and there were pieces rubbed off the ball by this metal bat so I complained. I was ready to complain if I thought I

had a chance of succeeding or if it was the right thing to do. And it was. Dennis got all shirty about it and eventually Greg Chappell strode on with his most upright and elegant walk carrying a bunch of bats, wooden bats, under his arm. The umpires had told Lillee he had to change his bat but it took Greg walking on to get him to do it. And then Lillee hurled it like a discus thrower 30 yards to the boundary and then got on with the game. Geoffrey Boycott was very annoyed with me because he said I was stirring Dennis up just before he came into bowl. And, indeed, he took four wickets for whatever it was [73 from 28 overs] and he got Boycott for 0 [lbw] and suddenly we were 41 for four. I think the actual aluminium bat sits in my son's house given to him by Dennis 10 years later and signed by all the players. It was one of the nice things about Dennis, you see. After that conflict and that big event he took the trouble to do that and get it signed and give it to my son.

DENNIS LILLEE: The alli bat was interesting. My business partner and I came up with it. It was his idea basically but we were in partnership in indoor cricket and one day he brought in this alli bat with a rough handle with some tape around it and said 'Have a hit with this.' That's how the idea started. He got the idea from the aluminium bats in baseball so it went from there to 'what a good idea.' Then we developed and we sold. We extruded a whole heap of metal, we made a dye or got one made up and then we extruded all this metal and we cut them down to size and taped them up.

> All of a sudden we're selling thousands of these bats both in men's sizes and children's sizes. We got a couple of approaches from bat manufacturing companies in England who would take over and give us a royalty. We thought, no, we're a bit smart for this we'll take the whole lot, thanks. So we told them where to go. Then the MCC banned them probably because of some tie-up with the bat companies. You saw what happened. I still hold the world record, I think, for the longest throw with an aluminium bat in a Test match. I can assure you that will stand. In the end I got Mike Brearley and his team to sign the bat and our team to sign it. On the top Mike Brearley put 'Good luck with the sales, Dennis. Mike Brearley.' Of course, that was the cerebral Mike saying basically 'It's all over, pal.' I've retained the bat and kept it in a safe place.

There is at least one aluminium bat outside the private collections of the Brearley and Lillee clans which is on display at the Bradman International Cricket Hall of Fame.

Divining greatness

Brearley, who provided Lillee with his 100th Test wicket during the 'alli Test', was returned to the leadership in dramatic circumstances in 1981 when Ian Botham resigned in advance of his inevitable sacking after two Ashes Tests. Burdened by the weight of expectation after being fast-tracked to the helm against Clive Lloyd's indomitable West Indians and in deep conflict with Sir Alec Bedser, the chairman of selectors, Botham did not win any of his

12 Tests as captain. When Lord's fell eerily silent after Botham made a pair in the drawn second Test against Kim Hughes's Australians, Brearley's return was inevitable. What was not anticipated was Brearley's ability to rehabilitate Botham in a trice.

> **IAN BOTHAM**: What was it like to be led by a psychotherapist? It was interesting because I used to love watching people meeting him [Brearley] for the first time. It's a bit like something off *Star Trek* because of his eyes—he's actually looking inside the head. I know this from the first time I really met him and I thought, well, he wasn't in there long with me. He worked it out very quickly—a very simple, very straightforward country boy. It is interesting for he really got under the skin of some of the opposition.
>
> If they'd got hold of him some of the Aussies would have ripped him apart because he just played mind games with them and invented words. I mean when Lennie Pascoe came along he called him a 'separatist', which of course went straight over the top. It was a great time. He wasn't the best player that ever played for England by any means and probably wouldn't get a start nowadays. But he was a magnificent captain and he did get the best out of the players.

That he divined the best in Botham is indisputable. A fortnight to the day after his public humiliation at Lord's, Botham's invincibility as an all-rounder was celebrated at Headingley, Leeds. With innings of 50 and an unconquered 149 and match bowling figures of 7–109, he had, along with Bob Willis, inspired a fantastic 18-run victory after England followed-on with a first innings deficit of 227. The only previous instance of a team winning after following-on was Andrew Stoddart's England tourists over Jack Blackham's Australians at Sydney in December 1894.

This was the fourth time in 38 Test matches Botham had scored a century and taken five or more wickets in an innings and it laid the foundation for what was destined to become known as Botham's Ashes. Three days earlier such euphoria was unimaginable. At stumps on day three England was 1–6 after Hughes had enforced the follow-on.

What followed instantly became part of the lore of Ashes cricket. At the end of the third day's play on July 18 the England team decamped en masse to Botham's home near Epworth in Humberside and, as David Gower has so succinctly put it, 'fell into a vat of beer'. What happens on tour does not always stay on tour and word soon spread that the team had backed up the following day, the Sabbath, at one of Botham's preferred watering holes, the Queen's Head in Epworth. After a very pleasant Sunday afternoon at the Queen's Head, team England returned to their hotel in Leeds and prepared to book out the following morning. Come Monday night they booked back in. Twenty-seven days later and after further feats of brilliance by Botham at Edgbaston and Old Trafford, England had famously secured the Ashes 3–1.

MIKE BREARLEY: As it happened I didn't get to the party as my wife was going to America and she was leaving in the middle of the night. So I didn't go. Was this a good call by the captain? It might have been. I don't really know as I never heard the full story about it.

IAN BOTHAM: It's all about preparation and rehydration. They just do it a bit differently now. I think I had more fun.

Duck season

Conspicuously absent from the Australian team so spectacularly defeated by Botham was Greg Chappell, one of the world's foremost batsmen of the time. A confluence of events caused Chappell to withdraw from the tour and Hughes to be returned to the captaincy. Chappell's state of mind had been widely and loudly questioned after he ordered his younger brother Trevor to bowl an underarm delivery to prevent New Zealand from an improbable win in a limited-over match in Melbourne earlier in the year. Furthermore, his absence on long tours since his Test debut in December 1970 had placed a great strain on his marriage and young family and he needed time to realign his priorities.

Inevitably, given the Ashes failure, he was immediately returned to the leadership and the extent to which his prowess was missed in England was graphically illustrated when he crafted his fourth double century in the second Test with Pakistan in Brisbane. To this point only Don Bradman (12) and Wally Hammond (7) had scored more double hundreds.

Yet barely a fortnight later his dismissal for a duck in the second innings of the third Test at the Melbourne Cricket Ground precipitated a collapse of confidence and form unthinkable for a batsman of such renown. Between 15 December 1981 and Australia Day 1982 Chappell made seven ducks in 15 Test and limited-over innings—five coming in seven outings in the first three weeks of the darkest period of his cricket life. His countless admirers the world over were transfixed by his fall into mediocrity and despair.

GREG CHAPPELL: In the end I worked out what the problem was but I wish I'd worked it out a few weeks earlier. Initially I thought it was a technical problem. I spent weeks trying to work out what was wrong with my batting when I realised it was totally in my mind. I was at a point where I had the difficulties of a young family and a business and playing cricket—keeping those three balls in the air was very difficult. I knew [wife] Judy was struggling with a young family with me being away so much and I was feeling that. I knew I wasn't ready to retire from cricket fully but I wasn't fully engaged. I knew then and I certainly know now that if you're a touch off against opposition of that calibre then you're going to struggle and I was more than a touch off.

I walked off the ground a couple of times—once at the MCG and once at the SCG—after first ball ducks and I remember looking back thinking 'What's wrong, I didn't see the ball.' It lasted a matter of weeks but it felt like many months and for some it probably felt like years. And the more people talk about it the more I feel like it went for years. Rudi Webster, who had been the manager of the West Indian team during

World Series Cricket, lived in Melbourne at the time and he waited until almost the end of the series against the West Indies before he came into the dressing-room. He said: 'Are you watching the ball?' I can't repeat what I said to him. 'No, no are you really watching the ball? I know you've had a lot of advice but when things get a bit quieter back at the hotel just think about it. Are you really watching the ball?' And it was back in the room at the hotel that I realised that I wasn't watching the ball. I was watching the general direction but not in the way that I'd always watched the ball and I realised that it was my mental state that was my problem. I wasn't doing my routine, I wasn't going through my mental and physical routine ball after ball. Mind you, when you're only there for one ball it's very difficult. I mean some of the media at the time thought I was not very nice to make the comment that I was actually batting quite well but just was getting out. And in the nets I was batting well. But obviously in the nets I wasn't having the anxiety. After the first ducks I started to get into that anxious state which becomes a never-ending spiral. Once I got back to my mental routine in the very next Test match against the West Indies in Adelaide it all turned around and I got 60 odd in the first innings. Unfortunately I had my hand broken in that innings by Colin Croft when I was about seven.

But despite the broken hand I felt really elated because I knew that I was back on track. The problem stemmed from the fact that I was not sure whether or not I should be playing. Then I had a conversation with Judy and my eldest son, Stephen, who would have been about seven at that stage. I asked him what he thought about my run of outs and he said: 'It's not very good. Why don't you play properly?' I thought that was a very good piece of advice so between Rudi Webster and Stephen I managed to sort it out.

High jinks

Doug Walters wore the appellation of 'the people's cricketer' with particular pride.

An uncomplicated soul he was in the minds of many the most popular Australian cricketer of a generation that also saw Ian and Greg Chappell, Dennis Lillee and Rod Marsh attain heady status in the wider community.

The 1970s was a time of social and political upheaval in Australia and the apparent casualness and irreverence of Walters struck a resounding chord, especially with those classified by demographers as belonging to Generation X.

He was a gifted and instantly likeable country fella whose predilections for beer, cigarettes and the punt simply added to his magic as an attacking batsman, thrilling fieldsman and useful change bowler.

Stories are legion of his smoking and drinking habits, his indifference to training and practice and the crossword puzzles or solitaire and cribbage that occupied his attention as he waited to bat.

He was cheered to the echo by his myriad fans, especially at his beloved Sydney Cricket Ground where the power of the people on the now defunct Hill eventually compelled the ground's governors to officially construct a Doug Walters stand in 1985. This remained the spiritual home of his most devoted followers until the redevelopment of the ground at the Randwick end and the establishment of the Trumper stand.

Walters was philosophical about the demolition of the stand and said he could not complain given that it was replaced with a bar. This was another observation which endeared him to his devotees who nearly 40 years later recall where they were the day their Dougie hit a six from the last ball of the day to score a century in a session against England in Perth.

Walters, one of the game's finest raconteurs, has vivid recall of the moment that will always hold a special place in the rich lore of the game.

> **DOUG WALTERS**: Greg Chappell got out just before tea. Normally, when two guys cross on a cricket field there are not many words spoken, just a 'good luck' and a 'bad luck'. But when Greg came through the gate he said: 'I got out so you can get 100 in the last session.' I didn't even say 'bad luck'. I just walked out on to the ground and a few minutes later it was tea and I was three not out. When I came back in I said: 'What do you mean you got out so I could get 100 in the last session? You wouldn't get out to give your mother a hit.' And he wouldn't! He said: 'We need some quick runs and you're the man.' You wouldn't believe how it turned out. I was batting with Ross Edwards at the time and at drinks, halfway through the session, I was pretty close to 70 and I

had views of being 130 or 140 at stumps. Ross, being an accountant could count from one to eight and I didn't face a ball for 27 minutes after drinks. Ross got a single off the eighth ball for four overs in a row and he'd done the same thing the last over before stumps and I was on 93 down the other end. The first ball of the next over he got hit on the pads and it just dropped straight down on his feet and I said: 'Get down the other end.'

So I was on 93 and the first ball I faced from [Bob] Willis was pitched short. He'd been averaging quite a few short-pitched balls and I got the top edge and it went straight over [wicketkeeper] Alan Knott's head for four, a couple of bounces into the sightscreen. I thought 'not a very convincing shot' but I'm on 97. I said he's going to give me another two or three short ones in the next six before the end of the eight-ball over. But he never gave me another one until the last one. I knew it was coming because he had a man behind square and he had another guy at fine leg. He'd been averaging four or five an over, anyway, and fast bowlers normally can't help themselves for that long. So, I decided that if he was going to give me a short one I was going to have a go. It was either him or me. And, fortunately, it went between those two guys on the leg-side and just over the ropes. So not quite in the Swan River where a lot of people think it ended up. Yes, it was a great moment. I ran off the ground as soon as I'd hit the ball not knowing whether it was going for four or six or I was going to be out. I knew it was the last ball of the over anyway. So I went running into the room thinking the boys might

> have the tops off a couple of bottles by the time I get there. But I run into an empty dressing-room. There was absolutely no one there. They were all hiding up in the ablution block. So I started to knock the tops off a couple of bottles and Ian Chappell appeared abusing me about getting out off the last ball. I said, 'Yes, good joke Ian, are you going to take the tops of these bottles or am I going to take them off?' He said: 'You shouldn't have got out. We needed some more runs tomorrow. I'm quite serious.' I whipped the tops off the bottles and the other blokes have got pretty good ears because they came running out when they heard the tops come off the bottles. And we knocked the tops off a couple more. The next day I was out second ball without adding to my overnight score and I came running back into the dressing-room and, oh, surprise, all the fellas were there. I went up to Ian Chappell and said: 'You don't put off to tomorrow what you can do yesterday.' I pulled a few tricks on the boys and that was just one of the occasions they got me back. They got me back on a few other occasions as well but I think it was a way of getting rid of the tension. You could be yourself and try and calm down the other guys.

For all his joshing of the accountant, at the other end the records show Edwards top scored with 115—the second of his centuries in a brief 20-Test career in which he averaged 40.37—and with Walters added 170 for the fifth wicket in a total of 481. It was the decisive stand of the match, enabling Australia a nine-wicket victory in a series they were destined to win 4–1.

Four years later at the height of the World Series Cricket schism both Walters and Edwards were unable to rekindle such form and confidence. They were so seriously out of sorts that their employer, media magnate Kerry Packer, insisted they have extra-curricular sessions at the cricket centre run by former England all-rounder Barry Knight in Kent Street in the heart of Sydney.

> **DOUG WALTERS**: My form during those two years of World Series wasn't all that good and Ross had similar problems. Kerry suggested to both of us that we had to fix things and after the first year [1977–78] he took us into Barry Knight's Centre. He said: 'Five o'clock Friday I want to see you blokes in at Barry Knight's.' So at five past five Kerry arrived and pulled off his suit jacket and started throwing balls at us from halfway down the wicket trying to knock our heads off. Barry Knight said: 'Hey, Kerry, hold on, you're going to kill one of these two guys.' And Kerry said: 'Well, what do you think I should do with them then?' Barry suggested tennis balls be thrown on a squash court to get the back foot defence in order. Kerry said: 'Okay, you two guys, book a squash court somewhere between where you live for an hour every Tuesday and Thursday. I'll look after the squash court.' So for the next six months we were at the squash court every Tuesday, every Thursday for an hour. And, you know, there wasn't one Tuesday or Thursday went by that Kerry didn't ring to find out whether we were there. I'm sure he wasn't worried about his two dollars a week that he was paying the

guy for the squash court. I thought he had a genuine interest in us so that was good.

High-flier

If Greg Chappell was the most graceful right-handed batsman of his day Englishman David Gower was the left-handed artist nonpareil.

And to the unbridled delight of the game's many aesthetes and romantics they once brought the matchless beauty of their batting to the same occasion, each scoring a century in the third match of the 1982–83 Ashes series. Appropriately, their canvas was the old charming, tranquil Adelaide Oval.

Gower occupies a unique place in the history of Anglo-Australian cricket. If the cold, calculating Bodyline captain Douglas Jardine is the English cricketer most loathed in Australia Gower can lay claim to being the most admired perhaps even openly loved.

Chosen for the first of his five tours to Australia at the age of 21 in 1978, he captivated crowds with his elegant and precise stroke play and, until his shoulder crumbled, his thrilling out fielding. Over the next 13 years he played 42 Tests against Australia and scored 3269 runs at 44.78 with nine centuries. It was in the white heat of Ashes cricket that he was at his alluring best and he was celebrated for it.

Thought by English critics to be the reincarnation of Frank Woolley—the celebrated English all-rounder for a quarter of a century from 1909—Gower was also fair, blue-eyed and handsome and possessed a quick wit and ready smile. In every respect he was a godsend for the game, which in the early years of his career was beset with the bitter residual resentments from the breakaway World Series Cricket movement.

To Australian crowds he was the very antithesis of the archetypal English professional. They recognised and celebrated his joie de vivre and on the odd occasion he ruffled the governors' feathers he had the crowd's wholehearted and vocal support. Gower did not take himself too seriously. He was an impulsive and sometimes impudent character who sometimes stirred the pot. And he was loved for it. That he liked a tipple, albeit bubbly rather than beer, also did him no harm in the eyes of the hoi polloi.

Certainly moral support was gratefully received during his final tour of Australia in 1990–91 when, for a lark, he went joyriding in a 1930s biplane Tiger Moth and buzzed his teammates playing against Queensland in a first-class game at Carrara on the Gold Coast. England won by 10 wickets but the hierarchy was not amused as Gower was playing in the match and had not sought permission to leave the ground.

> **DAVID GOWER**: Life is a very, very broad canvas and cricket has covered a lot of my canvas over the years. I always set out not to let it get me down and I've tried to keep a perspective on other things. You know, it's all very well being cast as a slightly flamboyant character, as flippant, as wine-loving, as good-living, as laissez-faire or as laid back. All these things are okay in some sort of moderation because you have to try and remember, and you have to convince people sometimes, that

the cricket is important. When I was accused of being too laid back for instance I would be at pains to tell people 'No, I'm not.' I sometimes portray that consciously as a way of . . . as a sort of self-defence mechanism to take the pressure off, as it were. In order to succeed and to make 8000 odd Test runs [8231 runs at 44.25 with 18 centuries] and all that sort of stuff you have to have a core of steel of some description. There has to be a firm base, there has to be an inner strength, there has to be a determination and there has to be a keenness to do well and I've got all that, I had all that. But I like to cover it up with other things as well and the Tiger Moth was part of that.

In the first three Test matches of that tour I top scored in both innings in Brisbane, although we hadn't made a lot of runs there, and I'd got hundreds in Melbourne and Sydney. I'm thinking I'm doing okay here but we're losing and you look at yourself and think if there is anything more you can do individually to help the team improve. The Tiger Moth . . . it was a fascinating insight into the way other people's minds worked and, I think, it's a great lesson for captaincy. My attitude to player responsibility is for players to think for themselves and the acknowledgement that everyone is different and that different people need different things to be good, to be at their best and to get the best out of themselves.

The attitude on the 1990–91 tour under Stewart [team manager Micky Stewart] and Gooch [captain Graham Gooch] was that every man was a machine. It was a communist regime; one size fits all. I couldn't abide that. After the incident at Carrara with the Tiger Moth I was called into the manager's suite in the morning. So with Peter Lush [tour manager], Micky Stewart and Graham Gooch and my one ally in the room, Allan Lamb as vice-captain, I was asked: Why, why did you do it? I said: 'If you really want to know that we're probably not going to get on here,' or words to that effect. It was just a little bit of fun, maybe misjudged, but harmless. I felt it was an opportunity that I couldn't miss—these two Tiger Moths doing regular tours of the ground at Carrara and heading off up the Gold Coast. I was thinking through lunch about the chance to get one of those up in the air and buzz the ground. I thought I've got to do this. I felt sorry for Johnny Morris who had made a hundred that day [132 while Gower managed 13] and overheard a conversation with Allan Lamb where I said I might just go and nick one of those planes for a moment. And he said: 'Can I come too?' It wasn't good for his career and it wasn't good for my career. But, as I say, it was just one of those things I had to do and there would have been a smile and a grin.

I've got the photographs of the whole escapade. I've got a wall full of cartoons that were drawn by all sorts of cartoonists in all sorts of newspapers and publications both in Australia and back in the UK. These are a happy reminder of what was a bit of fun. But on the back of it there was an hour-long discussion on motivation and team ethics and all the rest of it. To which my one response at the time was: Why are you worried about me? I've got runs in every game so far, I've got hundreds in Melbourne and Sydney and I haven't played much better than that ever. My Sydney hundred [123 from 236 balls in 312 minutes to take his aggregate beyond 8000 runs] was a thing I've treasured ever since. I loved every moment of it, was so proud of it and they had this long discussion about motivation with me. The correct response was: Why are you worried about me? What about the other 10? You know you've got a whole team to get motivated here, don't take it out on me.

The irony of the whole thing and the one thing that bugs me is that after paying the £1000 fine [the maximum possible under the tour contract] I could not get a run. Peter Lush agreed it was the end of the affair and all I wanted to do then was go and make more runs in exactly the same way. I had [Geoff] Boycott's record in my sights. I had all sorts of good reasons, incentives to play well for the rest of the tour and as I walked out to bat at Adelaide in the fourth Test match they put 'Those Magnificent Men in their Flying Machines' over the PA system, which kind of made me giggle. As I walked out I thought okay, refocus, but for some reason all form disappeared. I could not get a run. I mean, if you look at the scores in Adelaide [11 and 16] and Perth [28 not out and 5] in the final two Test matches—they are appalling. That's what really bugged me most about the whole affair. I didn't mind doing it and I've lived on it ever since and I've told the story a million times ever since. I've worked for the BBC on something called 'The Air Show' and I've flown Tiger Moths since for the BBC. You know it's stood me in good stead for the rest of my life and it always will do. The one thing that bugs me is that my form disappeared straight after and I couldn't just say: There you are, there's more runs, now will you leave me alone.

Double entendre

Broadcaster Jonathan Agnew knew perfectly well how Gower would have reacted to such a joyless period in a career which had brought such joy to his myriad followers the world over.

Agnew, who played under Gower's captaincy at Leicestershire and, on three occasions, for England, shared his skipper's sunny view of cricket life and smiled and laughed more often than is expected of a fast bowler.

> **JONATHAN AGNEW**: I played cricket like I talk about it and so I'd have a josh with the batsman, I'd joke with the umpire and go and sit on the fence at fine leg and talk to the crowd between balls. I just thought people didn't take me very seriously and I took it absolutely seriously. What's wrong with having a bit of fun about what you do? You know I hate seeing automatons running around grounds training.
>
> You know you've got to run this way or skip like that because you've been told to. I think of myself as a bit of a rebel sometimes which is why I loved playing cricket with David Gower. Dear David would quite happily just let you get on with it. I mean, once we took to the field with David as captain and 12 people because he hadn't thought about telling my mate Les Taylor that he wasn't playing. He said, 'Go on, Aggers. Set the field.' So three slips, gully, cover, mid-off, mid-on, short leg, fine leg, hang on.
>
> 'But David we've got 12 people out here.'
>
> And David said: 'Oh, well, Les, you're twelfth man' and

> sent him from the field. That was what playing with David could be like. I mean, he would hate me to say that was all it was like. It wasn't. The point being that he did let you think for yourself, make field settings and plans for batsmen and I loved to be treated as a grown-up rather than being told what to do all the time.

Despite impressive endeavours for Leicestershire in the latter part of the 1980s—including an exceptional 101 wickets in 1987—Agnew could not convince the selectors he was indeed a serious cricketer and worthy of further representative honours and at the age of 30 retired to realise his boyhood dream of broadcasting cricket on the radio.

He enjoyed a meteoric rise to prominence and in 1991, just months before the death of arguably the greatest of all cricket broadcasters, John Arlott, he joined the British Broadcasting Corporation's renowned Test Match Special team.

Any hopes he held of sharing with his audience precious insights into Gower were dashed when the hierarchy at Lord's imposed a penance on the former England captain for his attitude and antics on the Australian tour and ignored him for five Tests against the West Indies and a solitary Test against Sri Lanka.

The fifth Test with the West Indies at The Oval in London produced a moment in commentary that simultaneously lifted Agnew's on-air profile and entered the rich lore of the game. Furthermore it was destined to become a YouTube sensation and 22 years later is still a tonic and regularly visited.

Reviewing England's first innings, Brian Johnston, renowned

for his vaudevillian style at the microphone, referred to Ian Botham's unfortunate 'hit wicket' decision while batting against Curtly Ambrose. With his score at 31 Botham overbalanced and in attempting to step over his wicket accidentally removed a bail with his inner thigh and was given out.

'He just didn't quite get his leg over,' observed Agnew, tongue firmly implanted in reddening young cheek.

Johnston continued for a moment before sniggering and snorting: 'Aggers, for goodness sake, do stop it,' was all he could say.

Both were engulfed in paroxysms of laughter as Johnston attempted to tell of the exploits of unbeaten Chris Lewis and tailenders, Phillip DeFreitas and David Lawrence. It took some moments before they regained composure and the broadcast was continued in a more conventional manner.

The 'leg over' has been voted British broadcasting's most memorable sporting moment and it is said that countless drivers had to pull to the side of the road and stop because they were convulsed with laughter. Apocryphal or not it has been recorded that a two-mile traffic jam at the Dartford Tunnel outside London was caused by the incident.

> **JONATHAN AGNEW**: It had a huge impact on me because it was my first summer and it put me on the map, really. I was this new young lad who turned up so I think I was very lucky that so early on people could associate me with someone who liked a bit of a laugh. So you know people rather warmed to it and there was this relationship between Brian Johnston and me. We tried to broadcast three or four times and just failed

> to do it. It was hopeless with him giggling and chortling. So this thing went on, you see, so it really established me as a member of the team. It was very funny. But Johnners wasn't happy and at the end he stomped off. He thought he'd been unprofessional and he'd sounded terrible. But the next day when he played it back and he listened to it he could see how funny it was. I think he and I will always be bound together, as it were, by our leg over moment.

Agnew was at the microphone the following season when his great friend Gower was recalled for his last three Test matches before he too gravitated to broadcasting and began an outstanding career in television.

The little red savings book

Among Gower's closest allies in the broadcasting booth is Jamaican Michael Holding whose quiet demeanour and distinctive, mellifluous voice belie his history as the most fearsome and devastating of fast bowlers.

As with many of his contemporaries who have been drawn to media work at the end of a distinguished career in the middle, Holding is a wonderful raconteur.

All entertainers have their schtick and Holding can hold spellbound a crowd with his retelling of a meeting with deposed England captain Tony Greig just months after he offended the West Indian diaspora by boasting the English cricketers would make Clive Lloyd's 1976 West Indian team 'grovel'.

Holding, politically savvy and a friend of Jamaica's cricket-loving prime minister of the day, democratic socialist Michael Manley, was appalled by Greig's remark, which to him smacked of racism and apartheid.

Greig, a larger-than-life South African-born all-rounder given to hyperbole, soon rued his recklessness and was humiliated not once, not twice but thrice as the West Indies completed an emphatic 3–0 series victory in just four of the five matches. Holding, driven by his anger to bowl at furious speed, took 28 wickets at 12.71, including a phenomenal 14–149 at The Oval.

In March 1977, a week before the international cricket community focused attention on the fabulous Centenary Test between Australia and England at the Melbourne Cricket Ground, Lloyd's West Indian team took the lead in a five-match home series against Pakistan.

Much to his annoyance, 23-year-old Holding could not play because of a badly damaged right shoulder and he remained in Kingston, Jamaica to convalesce. He was not, however, left out of the loop as a seismic shift in the game started to take place. Lloyd, surrogate father to Holding and so many other aspiring Caribbean cricketers, saw to that.

> **MICHAEL HOLDING**: I'll tell you how it started. Lloydie called me from Trinidad and said to me: 'You know this thing is happening with Kerry Packer.' I had absolutely no idea who Kerry Packer was or what was going on. Lloydie said two people would come and see me because they wanted me involved but it was all hush hush. I said okay and asked him

if he had signed. He said 'Yes' and that Viv [Richards] was thinking about it. I asked who were the people coming to see me and he said: 'One is Austin Robertson and the other one is Tony Greig.' When he said Tony Greig the phone almost dropped out of my hand. I didn't want to see this man because of what had happened in England. Lloydie just said: 'Yes, but you just have to listen to him.'

They came to Jamaica and we met at the Sheraton Hotel and they showed me everything. And again I didn't have a clue what they were showing me—magazines, there was a magazine that Kerry Packer owned and the television station and they were showing me balance sheets which meant absolutely nothing to me. I just said: 'Listen, Lloydie has signed just show me where to sign.' And I signed. I didn't see myself as an occupational cricketer going to play for a very long time. I was actually at university because I'd gotten a four-year scholarship from the Jamaican government to do computer science so I saw myself heading in that direction anyway.

And secondly, which of course was quite personal and very selfish, when Kerry Packer sent these guys to see us we were explicitly told that we would still be able to play for the West Indies. I personally didn't think it might hamper England's cricket, or South Africa's cricket or Australia's cricket. I was thinking selfishly because here's this man offering so much more than I had earned in the series I'd just finished playing. I thought to myself well if this is money that I can go and play cricket for and if I am still able to play for the West Indies, that's even a bigger bonus. I was looking at it selfishly and had no problems signing. I thought to myself there's no way anyone is going to pay the sort of money they were talking about to play cricket.

I'd just finished playing a series against India in the Caribbean and then went to England to play a series there. Each Test match I played against India in the Caribbean I got $US200. So when someone comes to you and offers you a contract for three years at $25,000 per year! And this is not for 12 months—this is just the Australian summer and when the Australian dollar is bigger than the US. You have to think to yourself that they are mad or no such thing is going to happen. Greig and Robertson left and said I'd get one-third of the contract fee as soon as they got back to Australia. They said they were going around seeing other people and should be back in Australia perhaps in nine or 10 days and would wire the money. I didn't wait for the tenth day. On the ninth day I went to the bank and I gave the teller behind the counter my little savings book. You know in those days you had a savings book and I gave it to her and said: 'Can you update this savings book for me please?' She put the book into this machine they had in those days and it made a lot of noise and banged a few keys. Things were printed in the book and she handed it back and I opened the book and there was no money and I went home.

I told my parents about it obviously but I couldn't say anything to anyone else. So I thought to myself 'this is rubbish, this ain't happening, there is no way anyone is going to pay

> that sort of money for a cricketer. So, I wait a few more days and I go back to the bank again. I give the lady behind the counter my book again and I say: 'Can you update this savings book for me please?' And she goes bang, bang, bang, bang and pushes back the book. This time I opened the book and for the first time in my life I see a comma in my savings book. I had never had anything in my savings book getting into four figures because you talked about hundreds at that stage of your life. I thought, hell, this is really happening because there's no way they're going to send this money if it isn't happening. That's when I knew it [World Series Cricket] was really on.

Sharing the spotlight with the Don

Holding and his confreres were the scourge of batsmen the world over as the irresistible West Indies wrought havoc throughout the 1980s.

At Clive Lloyd's guiding hand and with ruthless efficiency the finest group of fast bowlers ever assembled inflicted extensive physical pain and mental scarring.

This was especially so of the elite batsmen of England and Australia, who were pounded into submission and very publicly made to know their place in the greater scheme of things. England lost 19 and won one of 28 Test matches between June 1980 and April 1990. Australia fared marginally better losing 12 and winning three of 21 Tests between December 1979 and February 1989.

Demoralisingly, 10 of the 21 matches for the Frank Worrell Trophy were played in 10 months from March 1984 and they took a dreadful toll on the Australians and especially Kim Hughes.

Hughes, on song one of the game's most dynamic batsmen, was broken by the relentlessness of the West Indian assault and managed just 294 runs at 21.00 in seven Tests and tearfully resigned the captaincy after two matches of the 1984–85 home series.

Border, who even as Hughes's deputy had not conscientiously evaluated the responsibilities of leadership, suddenly was propelled into the position he was destined to hold for 93 consecutive matches over the next nine years and three months.

And if his new commission as Australia's 38th captain was not challenge enough, he took over as the centenary of Test cricket at Adelaide Oval was celebrated before the majority of surviving Test captains to have led at one of the world's most beautiful grounds.

Among those who trained a critical eye on Border were Sir Leonard Hutton, Freddie Brown and Mike Smith (England), Lala Amarnath, Bishan Bedi and Chandu Borde (India), Trevor Goddard (South Africa), Bevan Congdon (New Zealand), Mushtaq Mohammad and Intikhab Alam (Pakistan) and Australians Sir Donald Bradman, Ian Johnson, Arthur Morris, Richie Benaud, Bob Simpson, Bill Lawry, Ian Chappell and Greg Chappell.

Having put his modest credentials before such august company at a celebratory dinner, he then had to share the podium with Sir Donald Bradman at his first team meeting as skipper.

ALLAN BORDER: We had this process where we had a team dinner, a very quiet dinner, just for the boys, and we had an invited guest. I'm about to do my first team meeting as captain so I'm a bit nervous, you know, about talking to the troops. I'm not a great speaker by any stretch of the imagination and I had to get up and rally the troops for this big effort against the West Indies. I think we were only 2–0 down at that point. So we were struggling for results. I'm in the room as the new captain and the invited guest is Sir Donald Bradman. So I had a double dose. I was nervous enough just talking to the blokes I knew really well about a big effort in the Test coming up the next day. But doing it in front of the great man I was doubly nervous. But to be honest he was fantastic. We talked a lot about our situation. He knew pretty much what we were going through—how difficult it was playing four fast bowlers, the relentless pressure that builds up.

We talked a lot about Bodyline [1932–33] and the similarities. He did make a lot of comparisons and was very up-to-date with his thinking. He was a very forward thinker, Sir Donald, so he gave us a lot of confidence. It was good to have those conversations with him flying around the table over dinner. He knew what we were going through—the difficulties of playing a side like the West Indies. It was good to get it from him. I can remember the initial situation and he was just sitting at the table waiting for this great, you know, oration from the new Australian skipper. And I'm thinking I don't need this pressure as well. But it was great that he was there. I've got to say it was a good couple of hours. It was brilliant to get a chance to talk with him in a very private situation.

Plod and Dasher

Arthur Morris was feted at the Adelaide Oval Centenary celebrations because he had deputised for the injured Lindsay Hassett for the third Test with John Goddard's West Indian team in December 1951 when Test cricket was played on Christmas Day for the first time.

At 91 Australia's oldest surviving Test cricketer in 2013, Morris is numbered among Australia's greatest batsmen and most charming sporting personalities.

An elegant left-hander who scored 12 Test centuries and had the distinction of outscoring Don Bradman in the Test matches of the Invincibles tour of England in 1948, he is also a marvellous storyteller who smiles readily and laughs heartily.

From his teenage years in the Great Depression Morris had ambitions to play cricket for New South Wales and Australia even if he was unable to afford his own bat.

Indeed, he used a bat from the St George District Cricket Club kit to score his first First Grade hundred in 1938–39 and again when at 18 he became the first player anywhere to record a hundred in each innings of his initial first-class match—against Queensland at the Sydney Cricket Ground in 1940.

To mark his achievement Doc Evatt, the cricket-loving politician and silk who was destined to serve as deputy prime minister to Ben Chifley and later lead the Labor Party, arranged for

Morris to buy a bat at Stan McCabe's sports store in George Street, Sydney.

As Morris matured as a cricketer and his star rose, bat manufacturers were keen to identify him with their brand and he never again wanted for a trusty blade. In fact, he did not buy a bat until he retired from the first-class game in the mid 1950s. And therein lies a tale.

ARTHUR MORRIS: I bought a bat and I played for Paddington. It was a nice bat and I got picked for the Prime Minister's XI to play against England [on 10 February 1959] in Canberra. [Lindsay] Hassett was playing in it too and I think he might have had a couple of gin and tonics because he said, 'I haven't got a bat.'

I'd got 79 and I said: 'Here, use mine.' And he went out there and it was embarrassing. He played at about half a dozen balls and missed them by about a foot. I'd just got out of the dressing-room and am standing with the prime minister Bob Menzies, who loved Hassett, and he said: 'Isn't that typical of Lindsay, what a wonderful, wonderful gesture.'

And I said: 'What's that sir?'

And he said: 'He's given his bat to a little boy in the crowd.'

I did say a couple of words that were a bit rude. 'But it was my bat, Sir!' I wasn't very impressed with it but the poor little kid came back after and got all the autographs on it. That was Hassett with that dead straight face.

I remember so well the last game in London in 1953. We were facing defeat in the last Test, which was the only match

> decided in the series. Jim Laker and Tony Lock were bowling and Lock had a habit of throwing his fast one. Lindsay and I are opening and I'm up the other end and I just looked at his straight face and suddenly he yells out: 'Strike one.' And the next one comes down and Tony throws his fast one again and 'Strike two,' says Lindsay. I'm starting to laugh and we're trying to save the game. I looked at Hassett, who looked at captain Len Hutton, who turned his back immediately. Then he came down to me when he started to hit the ball well and said: 'Why don't you get on with it, Plod.'
>
> And I said: 'I don't know, Dasher, I can't get the strike.' Or something like that. From then on when we wrote to each other it would be Dear Plod or Dear Dasher. That was the character he was. Wonderful.

(That the 1960 *Wisden Cricketers' Almanack* records Hassett borrowing an umpire's hat to catch Colin Cowdrey after he'd scored a century in the Prime Minister's game suggests Morris's suspicions about his great pal's sobriety were correct.)

Baggy green caps and a shrinking sweater

Arthur Morris also had the opportunity to captain Australia in an Ashes Test the summer of 1954–55 and as the *eminence grise* of Australian cricket, has long been warmly welcomed to the inner circle of English cricket and to Lord's in particular.

Making light of fading hearing and the need for a walking stick, in 2008 he happily returned to Old Blighty for the 90th birthday celebrations of his dear friend and greatest adversary, Sir Alec Bedser. Twenty-one months later, in his 89th year, he made the journey again but with a heavy heart to deliver a eulogy at a memorial service to the great English bowler at Southwark Cathedral.

A captivating personality who enjoys the contemporary game and is stimulated by the company of young cricketers, Morris served as a member of the Sydney Cricket and Sports Ground Trust and has a vast range of friends and acquaintances across the social spectrum in Australia and the UK. Certainly he is on first name terms with former Australian prime ministers the Honourable Bob Hawke and Honourable John Howard, their British counterpart Sir John Major and celebrated journalist and interviewer Sir Michael Parkinson.

Parkinson, a Yorkshireman who for a time opened the batting for Barnsley ahead of Geoff Boycott, surreptitiously entered the Australian cricket family through his mateship with renowned Australian cricketers and journalists Jack Fingleton and Keith Miller. Inevitably, both found their way on to his eponymous television show, Fingleton with considerably more success than Miller.

> **SIR MICHAEL PARKINSON**: Keith Miller epitomised for me everything that excites me about the game. And there was an aesthetic pleasure, too, in watching Miller. He was a graceful athlete as well as being an explosive one and he kind of represented for me all that glamour in the game. Being a Yorkshireman I was a fairly dour cricketer. You know we take

cricket very seriously and Miller, of course being an Australian, also took it seriously. But he managed to do it with a joie de vivre that you never much met in any other person. He was a great star.

I was lucky enough to meet him later in my life and he didn't let me down. He became a friend, and when I came to Australia, a mentor and a guide, and he was very kind to me. He took me around and introduced me to all kinds of wonderful people—Harold Larwood, Arthur Morris and Neil Harvey, all those greats. He was very accommodating and very, very kind and I was honoured to actually be in his company. I had Miller's sweater [together with two of Fingleton's caps], his last Test sweater, which he gave to me in this plastic bag standing outside a Tattersall's Club in Manchester. 'Here, have that, I don't want it anymore, nobody wants it,' he said. I said I couldn't take it but he insisted.

I took it home and we had a cleaning woman who shoved it in the wash and it came out looking like it had been on bonny Prince Charlie. She'd shrunk it and it was awful, irredeemable. It was terrible.

Of curtains and coconut shells

Charismatic England women's captain Rachael Heyhoe-Flint was so nervous and preoccupied negotiating cricket's holiest place she was oblivious to the portrait of Keith Miller and so many other legends of the game adorning the walls of the Long Room at Lord's.

The date was 4 August 1976 and fate decreed that a 60-over encounter between the finest women cricketers of England and Australia became the first women's game to be played at the hallowed ground.

Originally slated for Sunbury, the failure of the Middlesex County Cricket Club to reach a quarter final of the Gillette Cup limited-over competition enabled the match to be transferred and so take its place in the rich history of the game.

Coming exactly a week after she had famously batted for eight hours and 41 minutes for an undefeated 179 to save England from defeat in the third match of a drawn Test series at The Oval, Heyhoe-Flint was intent on not breaching protocols and at the same time earning the respect of the Marylebone Cricket Club and its exclusively male membership. The 1976 *Wisden Cricketers' Almanack* noted that the English skipper was 'visibly feeling her responsibility as captain'.

A woman of strength, purpose and vision, not in her wildest dreams could Heyhoe-Flint have imagined she was destined for fame as one of the first women admitted to membership of the club in 1999. And five years later she was feted as the first woman elected to the full committee and with characteristic charm and wit took credit for an eight-million pound refurbishment of the pavilions which included the hanging of spectacular curtains in the Long Room.

RACHAEL HEYHOE-FLINT: The day we played at Lord's was, apart from my rather long, boring innings to save England from Test defeat against Australia, the highlight as far as my cricketeing and playing career was concerned. There's something almost holy about Lord's and I was so nervous on the day we played. For once we were getting a huge focus of the world and cricket upon us and the last thing I wanted was for anything to go wrong. We had to be the best. It wasn't a schoolgirl's giggle match or anything. It was England against Australia at Lord's for the first time ever and I just didn't want anything to go wrong.

I remember driving in through the gates in an automatic car one-handed with a cine camera in the other hand. I mean, nowadays somebody would be filming me going in, wouldn't they? But I was filming myself going in through the great gates at Lord's. I didn't want to go in the wrong place, you know, because women at that stage weren't members. They even had a lady dressing-room attendant. The men had all been dismissed for the day. They said they'd been tidying it all up and got rid of dirty old cricket shoes and one of the newspapers referred to Denis Compton's old jock strap hanging up in there. I don't think it was, really, but never mind and there was a little bowl of roses on the sort of wash table in there and I thought that a nice touch.

I wanted to be first on the field and fortunately I won the toss and decided to field. We came down the two flights of stairs [from the dressing-room] and I thought nobody has actually told me if we're allowed to walk through the Long Room. That's the normal route—down the stairs and turn left through the Long Room. But I thought I daren't do that as women aren't allowed in the Long Room. Are we, the playing team, allowed? So while the crowd was waiting for us I was taking the England team through the door by the committee room because I didn't want to do the wrong thing.

I mean, wouldn't it have been awful if we'd been kicked out before we'd even got on the field? So it was a great day and I managed to be the first woman to go out to the pitch. I also wanted to be the last one off the ground and having beaten Australia [by eight wickets] I managed to do so as I was not out. So it was just the most wonderful day and a huge crowd turned up, a huge crowd for us—about 8500 to 9000. It was just a truly memorable day.

Heyhoe-Flint's infectious personality, innate communication and public relations skills perfectly complemented her exceptional sporting prowess and with the help of the wealthy British philanthropist Sir Jack Hayward the inaugural women's World Cup of cricket was held in 1973, two years ahead of the men's event. This was a sporting coup for the ages and lifted her public profile to an unprecedented height throughout Britain.

RACHAEL HEYHOE-FLINT: I was amazed that I was perhaps beginning to be known as the women's cricket captain. I was trying to market the whole game and I think perhaps indirectly I became the sort of voice piece for women's cricket and I was invited to appear on 'Question of Sport' and that type of thing. And then I was invited to the *Daily Express* sports award luncheon, which was the biggest occasion of its type of that time. Then I heard I'd been nominated and was going to receive an award for Sportswoman of the Year. I thought this was peculiar given there hadn't been a cricket tour this year. How on earth had this happened? It was shortly after I got married and I didn't realise that my stepson Simon was getting, buying and gathering as many copies of the *Daily Express* as he could. He was telling all his mates at school at King's College in Shropshire to go out and buy a *Daily Express* and to tell their parents to do the same. They were just filling in applications . . . voting for me as Sportswoman of the Year.

So I'm sitting there during the luncheon and don't think I will get it and suddenly my name is called out. And I'm thinking, oh my God and I had to go up onto the platform and Princess Anne was there. I made this stumbling speech and I'm thinking what do I say? I said: The polite question that I'm always asked is: What protection do women cricketers wear? So I thought I had better reveal this to her royal personage, who was sitting with Jackie Stewart, the Formula One racing driver world champion and Sir Max Aitken, the chairman of the *Daily Express*.

So I said: 'Well, it's pretty obvious, you know. We wear coconut shells, you know, two if you're shy and three if you're very nervous.' I sort of blurted this story out without thinking. Princess Anne roared with laughter and the next day the front page picture of the *Daily Express* was the most wonderful picture [of Princess Anne] roaring her hind leg off. And you can practically see Jackie Stewart's tonsils and all because of the coconut shells. It was curious because as a result of that I started being asked for even more things on television and quiz programmes and chat shows and that type of thing. So it obviously paid off wearing coconut shells.

Bet your bottom dollar

Genial West Indian fast bowler Joel Garner underwent a mammoth growth spurt as he approached his 17th birthday in 1969 at the very time the first episode of the American children's television series *Sesame Street* went to air.

He grew nearly 13 centimetres during a long vacation and when he returned to school his contemporaries instantly afforded him the sobriquet of 'Big Bird'. And 'Big Bird' or, simply, 'Bird' he has remained to his myriad admirers the world over.

While mercifully he stopped short of Big Bird's 249 cm (8 ft 2 in) for a decade from 1977 he towered over the game as one of the most menacing and guileful of bowlers at a head-turning 203.2 cm (6 ft 8 in).

From an early age Garner was infused with the rich culture of Barbadian and West Indian cricket and his development was overseen by some of the greatest of the island's cricketers—fast bowlers Manny Martindale, Charlie Griffith, Wes Hall and the incomparable Sir Garfield Sobers among them.

Like all boys growing up on the island idyll he dreamed incessantly of playing cricket for the West Indies against the world's greatest players. Disappointed not to be chosen to play for the West Indies' youth team against Ian Chappell's Australian visitors in 1972–73, he at least managed to make the acquaintance of some of the visitors—Greg Chappell in particular.

JOEL GARNER: I was 20 and I was unlucky not to make the youth team so I watched the game and supported the other fellows. After the game the Australians were boarding the bus and it was at that point I had the opportunity to speak to Greg Chappell and a few Australians on the team bus. I had swapped a $2 Barbados bill for a Jamaican $2 bill with one of the Jamaican players and I asked Greg Chappell if he would sign it for me. I got four signatures on it—Greg Chappell, Ian Chappell, Dennis Lillee and Ian Redpath. On the other side I only had Clive Lloyd on it from the West Indies team.

I said to him: 'You see this $2 bill; this is going to haunt you', or words to that effect. 'I'm going to play against you and give you some trouble and remind you that you signed my $2 bill outside of Kensington Oval.' He just said: 'And you might, too.' I think, about eight or 10 years later I took it out of my wallet and said: 'Do you remember this?' He said it was definitely his signature and I told him I was the scrawny fellow who had asked for his autograph all those years before. I still have the bill to this day. I think that being that close, being able to talk to him, to get an autograph from him, could have been the changing point for me.

Afterword

The game of cricket, its players great and small and its dedicated followers have shown an admirable steeliness and resilience. This has been emphatically demonstrated over the past 35 years, as the game has convulsed time and again and sorely tested the faith of the true believers while simultaneously seducing their children and grandchildren.

Cricket has evolved at breakneck speed since the World Series Cricket revolution of the late 1970s and again revealed its unique capacity to adjust to the moods and mores of society at a given point in time. The game reflects society, as the distinguished English cricket writer and commentator John Arlott sagely observed.

Administered from the United Arab Emirates across the Arabian Sea from its 21st-century powerbase, India, the once conservative game of the British Empire is played in various forms as a popular entertainment attracting billions of dollars of investment from voracious commercial and media interests the world over.

Consequently, given the riches and the extent of change, there has been controversy and corruption yet, overwhelmingly, the most influential voices respect the time-honoured values and virtues of the traditional game.

By its celebration of the game's history and a commitment to education, the Bradman Museum and International Cricket Hall of Fame seeks to reinforce cricket's moral code.

As the content of the previous pages attest, cricket in all its forms has always represented much more than a game.

With characteristic warmth, Joel Garner, the much-loved West Indian 'Big Bird' observed: 'I think if you played cricket at the top for 10 years and you didn't have friends from the teams that you played against you'd have wasted 10 years of your life.'

This is a sentiment that bears repeating.

Acknowledgements

It has been a privilege to interview many of the world's foremost cricketers for the Bradman Museum and International Cricket Hall of Fame and their wholehearted support for the establishment of this unique interview archive to broaden its educational message is greatly appreciated.

The ambitious project was the brainchild of Mr Michael Ball, AM, who was the chairman of the Bradman Foundation when the Museum expanded to include the International Cricket Hall of Fame in 2010.

His successor Mr Maurice Newman, AC, and the indefatigable executive director of the Foundation, Ms Rina Hore, continue to ensure the integrity of the ongoing venture. Foundation patron Richie Benaud's imprimatur is a generous foreword.

Museum curator David Wells provided wise counsel and direction and, along with Ross Barrat, was prepared to move into the interviewer's chair if required. Cindy Pryma's resourcefulness at the photographic desk has been invaluable, as has Karen Mewes coordination of our travel requirements.

Sean Mulcahy was behind the camera in Australia, India, England and the Caribbean, while Michael Van Vuuren had the responsibility in South Africa. In India, Carlton Saldanha was a heaven-sent guru.

The herculean task of transcribing the interviews was willingly undertaken by Helen Mulcahy, who was ably supported by a clutch of diligent volunteers at the Museum.

Publishers Allen & Unwin have always cared deeply about cricket and cricket publishing and I have been grateful for the expertise and encouragement of Patrick Gallagher, Robert Gorman, Siobhan Cantrill and Angela Handley.

Mike Coward
Sydney, June 2013

Photo credits

TEXT PAGES

p. x: Bradman Museum
p. 11: Bradman Museum
p. 12: Viv Jenkins/Bradman Museum Trust Collection
p. 72: Philip Brown (top); Mike Bowers/Fairfax Media (bottom)
p. 122: Newspix (McCosker); Agence France-Presse (Kumble)
p. 166: Philip Brown
p. 195: Mike Coward
p. 196: Bradman Museum Trust Collection
p. 222: Newspix

FIRST PHOTO SECTION

p. 1: Philip Brown (top); Viv Jenkins/Bradman Museum Trust Collection (bottom)
p. 2: Viv Jenkins/Bradman Museum Trust Collection (top); Getty Images (bottom left); Howard Burditt/Reuters/Picture Media (bottom right)
p. 3: Philip Brown (top); Getty Images (bottom)
p. 4: Viv Jenkins/Bradman Museum Trust Collection (both)
p. 5: Bradman Museum (top); Viv Jenkins/Bradman Museum Trust Collection (bottom)
p. 6: Philip Brown (both)
p. 7: Philip Brown (all)
p. 8: Viv Jenkins/Bradman Museum Trust Collection (top); Philip Brown (bottom)

SECOND PHOTO SECTION

p. 1: Newspix (top); Philip Brown (bottom)
p. 2: Philip Brown
p. 3: Philip Brown (top); Viv Jenkins/Bradman Museum Trust Collection (bottom)
p. 4: Philip Brown (top left); Viv Jenkins/Bradman Museum Trust Collection (top right); Getty Images (bottom)
p. 5: Viv Jenkins/Bradman Museum Trust Collection (top); Philip Brown (bottom)
p. 6: Philip Brown (both)
p. 7: Philip Brown (top left and bottom); Cricket Australia (top right)
p. 8: Newspix (both)

Index to names

Page numbers in **bold** indicate player entries in 'Chapter two—The cast'
Page numbers in *italic* indicate photographs